POETRY REVIEW

WINTER 1999/2000 VOLUME
EDITOR PETER FORBES
ASSISTANT EDITOR STEPHEN T[...]
ADVERTISING LISA ROBER[T]

CONTENTS

And So Farewell
pages 3 – 17
Editorial; extract from Simon Armitage's *Killing Time* (4); interview with, and poems by, Mark Halliday (7); John Whitworth's sonnet history of the twentieth century (13); Roddy Lumsden on two anthologies of the century (14); poem by Helen Kitson (16); the Classic Found Poem (17)

A Second Look
18 – 20
Andy Croft on Randall Swingler

Poems
20 – 29
by Colette Bryce, Ian Parks (21), Sarah Wardle, Philip Gross (25), John Kinsella (27), Lawrence Sail (28)

The Review Pages
30 – 35
Bernard O'Donoghue on Heaney and Hughes' new translations of myth; Carol Rumens on Carol Ann Duffy (33); Ian McMillan on Roger McGough (34)

Poems
36 – 43
by Brian Jones, Alison Brackenbury (37), Bob Rogers (39), Bob Kaven (40), Patty Scholten (41), Peter Armstrong (42), Alan Brownjohn, Smita Agarwal (43)

Reviews
44 – 50
David Wheatley on Kathleen Jamie; William Scammell on the *Oxford Book of English Verse* (45); Iain Bamforth on Thomas Lovell Beddoes (48); Katherine Gallagher on Tracy Ryan (49)

Poems
50 – 61
by Tracy Ryan, John Gallas (51), Lola Haskins (52), Robert Saxton (54), Susan Wicks (56), Selima Hill (57), Vernon Scannell (58), Ros Barber (59), Dennis O'Driscoll (60), Gael Turnbull (61)

Reviews
62 – 72
Sarah Wardle on Nick Drake; Paul Groves on *The Forward Book of Poetry 1999* (63); Neil Powell on Adam Thorpe, Gillian Clarke, Herbert Lomas and Blake Morrison (64); Elaine Feinstein on Russian poetry (67); Gillian Allnutt on Maxine Kumin (68); Kwame Dawes on Marcia Douglas, Ishmael Fiifi Annobil and Jack Mapanje (69)

Poems
72 – 76
by Richard Kell, Anne Gray (73), Jane Holland (74), Carmine Starnino (75), Kevin Murray (76)

Reviews
77 – 81
Dennis O'Driscoll on Allen Ginsberg and Adrienne Rich; Kwame Dawes on Langston Hughes (79);

Poems
81 – 85
by John Gallas, Sheenagh Pugh (82), Anthony Howell (84), John Greening (85)

Reviews
86 – 93
Rod Mengham on John Ashbery; Ian McMillan on John Kinsella (87); Conor Kelly on Peter Fallon, Bernard O'Donoghue, Conor O'Callaghan, Vona Groarke, Gerard Fanning, Brendan Kennelly and Brendan Cleary (88); Robert Potts on *The Message* and *Oral* (92); poem by Siân Hughes

Endstops
94 – 96
News, Comment, Letters

All illustrations by Gerald Mangan

LONDON MAGAZINE

FICTION * MEMOIRS * CRITICISM * POETRY
CINEMA * ARCHITECTURE * PHOTOGRAPHY
THEATRE * ART * MUSIC

'A fantastic magazine whose place in the history of 20th century literary life grows ever more secure and significant' – *William Boyd, Evening Standard*
Each issue contains over 50 pages of poems and reviews of poetry.

NEW LME POETRY

Herbert Lomas *A Hopeless Passion*

Ted Walker *Mangoes on the Moon*

Robert Conquest *Demons Don't*

Nikos Kavvadias *Wireless Operator*

Three Finnish Poets, £7.95 each

Soon and recently in London Magazine
Tom Pickard Memoirs
Poems by Hugo Williams, Tom Paulin, Alistair Elliott, Philip Gross, John Montague, Vernon Scannell
Subscriptions:
£28.50 p.a. (six issues) to 30 Thurloe Place, London SW7

Single copies £5.99 from discriminating bookshops

EDITORIAL AND BUSINESS ADDRESS:
22 BETTERTON STREET, LONDON WC2H 9BU

telephone 0171 420 9880
email poetrysoc@dial.pipex.com
website http://www.poetrysoc.com

fax 0171 240 4818
ISBN 1 900771 19 5
ISSN 0032 2156

POETRY REVIEW SUBSCRIPTIONS

Four issues including postage:

UK individuals £27
Overseas individuals £35
(all overseas delivery is by airmail)
USA individuals $56

Libraries, schools and institutions:
UK £35
Overseas £42
USA $66

Single issue £6.95 + 50p p&p (UK)

Sterling and US dollar payments only. Eurocheques, Visa and Mastercard payments are acceptable.

Bookshop distribution:
Signature
Telephone 0161 834 8767

Design by Philip Lewis
Cover by Stephen Troussé

Typeset by Poetry Review.

Printed by Grillford Ltd at
26 Peverel Drive, Bletchley,
Milton Keynes MK1 1QZ
Telephone: 01908 644123

POETRY REVIEW is the magazine of the Poetry Society. It is published quarterly and issued free to members of the Poetry Society. Poetry Review considers submissions from non-members and members alike. To ensure reply submissions must be accompanied by an SAE or adequate International Reply coupons: Poetry Review accepts no responsibility for contributions that are not reply paid.

Founded 24 February 1909
Charity Commissioners No: 303334
© 1999

The Poetry Society is supported by BT

AND SO FAREWELL TWENTIETH CENTURY

by Peter Forbes

It would be good if all the Millennium hoo-ha resulted in a poem that caught the mood of the world on the cusp. As the year went on it seemed increasingly unlikely that it would happen. In most things these days the spirit is willing but the flesh that shifts the pen is weak. But, at the last minute, Simon Armitage has produced his poem-for-the-Dome, *Killing Time*, commissioned by the Poetry Society as one of its Poetry Places schemes, and now published by Faber (£6.99, ISBN 0 571 20360 4). Armitage was the obvious man for the job, with his topicality, his interest in cosmology, the deeper currents, and his rhythmic control.

The poem alternates long discursive cantos with crisp epigrammatic quatrains. The model for the long passages is MacNeice's *Autumn Journal*, an audacious move, second only to taking *The Waste Land* or *Four Quartets* as your template. It works because MacNeice's mood was itself millennial rather than merely a snapshot of 1938, and Armitage has a similar range, from an empathy with the detritus of quotidian life to a penchant for riddling metaphysical rumination.

The poem takes in events of the year such as the Colorado school massacre (brilliantly told in the conceit of bullets transformed into flowers), the Paddington railcrash, the balloon circumnavigation of the globe, the eclipse. The world that is too much with us jostles with the cosmic long view, and the result raises the tone of the Millennium celebrations considerably (unlike the Dome's own brochure – "Visit a larger than life school corridor"; "Observe British interior scenes: the garden shed, lounge and teenager's bedroom").

Another good omen for the Millennium is that it is now relatively easy to buy a Mark Halliday book in the UK. His third collection *Selfwolf* arrived too late for a full review but it is published by University of Chicago Press who do have distribution here. It might be hard to find in bookshops but it's available from amazon.com at £6.63 (ISBN 0 2263 138 40).

Selfwolf seems pretty clearly Halliday's best book so far. A recent article about the Bridget Jones phenomenon talked of her "recognition humour". Halliday's poetry works the seam of recognition pathos. He's a lucky man in his subject matter because American life is cluttered with things to recognise. So he reaches for the universals: love, loss, time passing, identity and yolks them to the heterogeneous sprawl of American life. In 'Removal Request' he laments that too many objects have stored memories of his life: shirts, pillowcases, "two books I carried on lunchbreaks in the summer of '81"; he dreams of the great clearance in cadences reminiscent of Auden's 'The Sea and the Mirror': "O Lord of silence, Chief of Unloading Unlimited / send viewless unprecedented nymphs / who'll kidnap me to a vast white casino...". He has a Hopperesque preoccupation with urban desolation – "On Narrangasett Boulevard there is / a black gas tank with iron stairs on it. / One could climb these stairs on a rainy night / and stand cold on the black top".

Halliday plays the novelist *manqué*, constantly inventing scenarios: it's the pattern people and things weave that interests him most, the place where the possible hardens into what actually happened, where "History / flowed from its vast sewer out though the hot weather". The whole is a little bit like Philip Larkin meets Frank O'Hara – it's the most refreshing poetry we've seen for a very long time. You can read more about the man on page 7.

> A recent article about the Bridget Jones phenomenon talked of her "recognition humour". Halliday's poetry works the seam of recognition pathos. He's a lucky man in his subject matter because American life is cluttered with things to recognise.

SIMON ARMITAGE
FROM: KILLING TIME

     Meanwhile, hot air rises.
And the two men held for twenty-one days in living conditions
        decidedly worse
than those in most high security prisons
        are not the victims
of some hard-line, oppressive regime, or political refugees,
        or eco-warriors
digging in on the side of rare toads and ancient trees,
        or dumbstruck hostages,
or Western tourists kidnapped by gun-toting terrorists,
        or moon-eyed murderers
on death row, or self-captivated Turner Prize exhibitionists,
        but balloonists, actually,
jet-streaming the globe, riding the one, continuous corner
        of the world's orb.
In a picnic basket swinging from a bunsen burner
        suspended beneath
a tuppeny rain-hood filled with nothing but ether,
        Messrs Piccard and Jones
hitched a ride on a current of air and lapped the equator
        in less time than it takes the moon
to go through its snowball-cycle of freezing and thawing.
        Think of all the mental energy
and tax dollars pumped into that Stealth bomber thing
        with its invisible paint
and silent engines and non-reflective angles;
        all that fuss
when all along we could have sided with the angels.
        All we have to do,
apparently, is catch the breeze and hold our breath,
        strike a match
and watch the planet going round and round beneath.
        All right, in practice
it wasn't a cakewalk. Stowed away within the microclimate
        of the capsule
was at least one mosquito that drew blood from both pilot
        and co-pilot,
and one of the two had to spacewalk the outside of the canopy
        snapping off icicles,
and not for Scotch on the rocks but as a matter of buoyancy.

    Nevertheless, could those men
who emerged stunned and smelly, who were hoping to land,
    touchingly, in the lap
of the Sphinx, rather than being dragged through sand
    to the back of beyond,
could they be representative of some higher and finer ideal?
    We could do worse,
couldn't we, than balloon? Could do worse than peel
    the skin from the soul
and dither and drift in the miles of airspace between heaven
    and Earth, could do worse
than quit the sink estates and the island tax-havens,
    look down cartographically
on town and country, golf-blight and deforestation,
    the veins and arteries of roads,
the blood-clots of traffic lights and service-stations.
    Could do worse, surely,
than clink glasses, balloonist to balloonist, mid-air,
    over invisible borders,
over East Timor, Rwanda, Eritrea,
    catch the breeze
and exchange personal gifts as tokens of good fortune,
    thrown basket to basket.
Forget flags on sticks, dolls in national costume.

    We could do worse
than idle, unprotestingly, where jets might otherwise fly,
    lounge on the flightpaths,
occupy no more than one balloon's-worth of sky, and not be tied
    to any plot of land.
We could do worse, could we not, than only cool and drop
    for supplies and fuel,
scoop snow with bare hands from mountain tops,
    make fingertip friends
in passing, occasionally jump ship to have sex or make love
    and generally
rise like thought bubbles without words into worlds above,
    be aerial and detached
over Kosovo, Pristina, let the wind be the driving force,
    let each bauble and blimp
be free and etherial, find its own way, follow its own course,
    could do worse
than tilt in the frozen light above the weather

and every night
be part of the solar system, blissfully clear-headed, whatever
    the state of play on the ground.
Be quiet and listen. From up there in the gods
    a person can hear
a nightjar winding its watch for morning, contented bullfrogs
    farting and snoring.
Balloons, like kindly, fat maiden-aunts in their new frocks
    walking home from a wedding,
like the cows coming in, the sighting of slow, gentle yachts.
    We could do worse
than hang around up there, thoughtful and vacant at once,
    while all unstable elements lapse
to a steady state, while gaps and partitions are given the chance
    to meet and mend,
while wounds heal, battlefields go to pot, weapons to rust.
    Impossible of course,
but couldn't we just, couldn't we just?

Announcing a new book of poems

Against Perfection

RICHARD BURNS

A truly European poet who integrates the paradoxes of his origins (Jewish, English, East European) in a unique personal voice. A poet in the Greek sense of the term, whose stylistic versatility brilliantly serves the diversity of his inspiration.

85 pp. £7.95
King of Hearts Publications
Fye Bridge Street, Norwich NR3 1LJ
Email: kingofhearts@paston.co.uk

Join us on the crest of a wave

from 2nd-7th May 2000
at Wells-next-the-Sea
for our third Poetry-next-the-Sea
a festival of poetry, music
and visual art

For further details, or to become a friend of the festival, contact the Festival Office:

**Helen Flanagan
Rowans, Waltham Road
Wells-next-the-Sea, Norfolk
NR23 1NE
01328 710193**

Reality USA

PETER FORBES INTERVIEWS MARK HALLIDAY

PF: Could you tell us a bit about "your" America – where you come from and your upbringing?

MH: My father got a Ph.D. in English at the University of Michigan, with a dissertation on Hemingway, and when I drifted into a Ph.D. program at the age of twenty-eight, in 1977, at Brandeis University, it was with a feeling of accepting an inevitable (and mostly happy) fate. My father was a minister's son who rebelled vigorously and my mother turned against her conservative Canadian parents, and so my brother and I were raised to be agnostic and leftist liberals. We grew up in Raleigh, North Carolina till I was thirteen (my father taught at N.C. State), and then in a Connecticut suburb of New York when my father became an editor of an American history magazine. Always a safe suburban kind of life, I'm afraid to say more as the reader may pick up another journal or a Roddy Doyle book.

PF: How did you get into poetry?

MH: Multiple causation, of course: felt mysteries of spirit itching to be externalized; wanted a kind of literature Daddy wasn't so sure about; wanted to impress Cathy (first girlfriend in college) who discovered Yeats alongside me; wanted a kind of "work" not easily measurable by all the practical efficient guys; found a hypnotic fascination in Yeats, and in short poems by Frost, Eliot, Stevens, Keats; began to suspect that many publishing poets were full of pomp-gas, and found this quite encouraging; and wanted some way to feel not totally unlike Bob Dylan.

PF: How does poetry fare on campus in the USA these days?

MH: On campus? Well, there are hundreds of little kingdoms, creative writing programs in which the head poet builds a myth around himself or herself. Hundreds of quarterlies published at universities. In one sense poetry is booming, thriving, while at the same time everyone feels terribly under-noticed.

PF: You said when we published you that it made you feel "internationally viable". Is it easy for American poets to feel non-viable?

MH: It's always easy for any artist to feel non-viable, I guess. I think American poets have no clue about how they might ever get themselves read in England, or in any other country besides our own. In this respect the world doesn't feel much like a global village. But maybe the Web will change all this?

PF: The American poetry scene appears very fragmented to us. Do you think you belong in any categorizable group? Do Ashbery and the New York School mean much to you?

MH: Fragmented indeed. Even if we all wanted unity, which we don't, the sheer overload of required reading would prevent it. There is always the fear of disappearing in the crowd, and bonding together with a group or team or movement seems like a way to escape disappearing. The groups that announce themselves always seem pathetic/hilarious to me – can't wait to see the teeshirts! – and then there are the ones mainly invented by journalists who, understandably, seek order through groupings. "New York School" is a silly yet now indispensable way of pointing to some shared attitudes of O'Hara, Ashbery and Koch and their younger admirers. When I try to locate myself on the po-map, I mention O'Hara and Koch, but not Ashbery. O'Hara and Koch helped me see, when I was in my twenties, that poems could be very smart and very talky and very funny *and* serious all at once.

PF: 'Reality USA' might be your central poem in its fictionality, heroic bathos, and your search for ACTUALITY. You seem to love fictionality: inventing plausibly real scenes – "Arby's Roast Beef" and Donna (or Nadine), the waitress in 'Reality USA'. There seems an almost religious awe in the face of quotidian reality.

MH: 'Reality USA' probably is a central Halliday poem, yes. It's about the anxiety of sensing that the world is incredibly rich and the fear of being unable to respond enough, to participate enough. When I invent little scenes of American life it's to give myself the sensation of having "dealt with" or "disposed of" a particular kind of vivid disturbing reality even though I haven't actually been there. Images of unreachable attractive women out there are a notable category. I'm not sure about the religious awe. But I certainly have that nervous feeling that everything is always going away and needs to be saved into language.

PF: You seem to be offering a new take on the overload of the consumer society – you deal with this explicitly in 'Describers'. Most poets doesn't seem to see this as a subject for poetry – do you see this as a *terra incognita* for poets?

MH: I think many American writers now have the sense that the overdose of stimuli constantly peppering one's mind – from TV, movies, magazines, newspapers, slick-looking books, the Internet – is a subject, an issue, a force shaping us and which we need artistic responses to. No doubt writers and other artists in 1959 felt the same thing, and in 1929 too – but there is some point at which a quantitative change does become a qualitative change. Today an intelligent alert person cannot ever escape the sense that you could "consume" words and images twenty-four hours a day, intelligently and alertly, and still miss infinities of equally interesting stuff. This awareness is exhausting and produces defences – varieties of irony and cynicism. So, there are quite a few American poets who think they are offering the needed artistic response to all this. Some of the Language Poets think they're doing it. Admirers of Ashbery think he's doing it. I've tried to do it in a few poems. I have a nagging hunch that there's some rock group that's doing it brilliantly but I haven't found out about them. We're going to want poets who seem to have "surfed" the electronic media very extensively without drowning, without losing identity and reflectiveness and courage; I wish I knew what their poems will look like.

PF: Your work seems like a poetic equivalent of Nicholson Baker's fiction – the minutiae, the sense of sexual awe ("lust seems such a fierce hairy word"). Do you agree and are there any other US novelists you especially relate to?

MH: I haven't read many pages of Nicholson Baker, but I've admired the maniacally detailed footnotes. One response to the impossible overload of contemporary reality is to locate terribly small areas of concern and then examine them with fanatical thoroughness.

I think Don DeLillo is great. *White Noise* and *Libra* and *Great Jones Street* all impressed me very much; he is deep into the ironies of a hyper-self-conscious hyper-technologized global-capitalist life. I could never acquire the authority, or even the mock authority, to depict vast arrays of social behavior (government, business, crime) the way DeLillo does, or Thomas Pynchon. Pynchon can be boring, but there is always the suspicion that his *next* thing will be fabulous.

Earlier this year I tried to fall in love with Will Self, but failed. The stories seemed too willing to be just clever/witty.

PF: Your poetry reminds me a little of a poet you probably won't know, the English poet Rosemary Tonks: a poetry of exclamation, lurid revelation, self-dramatisation. It's a mode, with French roots, that has never caught on here. Do you have a sense of European roots or are the antecedents specifically American?

MH: Rosemary Tonks sounds intriguing and I wish I knew about her. Shopping around for antecedents, as one does, I've been delighted by Apollinaire's 'Zone', and a good deal of Stevie Smith, and of Philip Larkin – but I guess my twentieth-century influences are almost all American. (But also Hardy, Yeats, Lawrence...)

PF: Who were the American influences?

MH: When I think about my influences, it seems as if anti-influences were equally important – I mean, poets whose work struck me as the WRONG WAY – "I'm not sure what I should do but I sure as hell don't want to do that". In the Seventies (my twenties) my poetic identity was very unstable and cloudy but I felt increasingly skeptical about the so-called Deep Image poetry which was a huge vogue then (Merwin, James Wright, Bly, Strand, Kinnell, and many runners-up) – that stock vocabulary of archetypes (stone, bone, blood, light, water) seemed all too easy to parody. So I was intrigued by anyone who indicated that in poems you could talk, think, argue, joke, tease, reconsider; and anyone whose subject matter included actual streets, buildings, cars, records, beverages.

The crucial event for me was meeting Frank Bidart. His poetry includes a strong element of earnest thinking-on-the-page or "thinking out loud" (albeit in a more agonized way than my way) – the sense that the poem is THE PLACE where the drama of a search for truth is happening. In this respect, and also in many matters of critical taste, Bidart immediately became a tremendous force in my life from 1978 on. Through him I met Robert Pinsky and Pinsky became an influence – both his poetry and his mid-Seventies book *The Situation of Poetry* which exposed the emptiness of much Deep Image writing. Also thanks to Bidart I read Robert Lowell more carefully than before and appreciated better Lowell's achievements of deceptively casual symbolic force in *Life Studies*. Like any grad student, I was feverishly ready for influences then, and during my years at Brandeis (1977-1982) I finally read Whitman (having been oblivious of him before!), and read Eliot and Frost and Stevens more carefully than before. Influence for me came in that stream (meanwhile not Pound, not Olson, not Duncan, not Creeley, not Levertov, not Zukofsky...). I read Hart Crane and decided he was a very charismatic failure. I loved Ginsberg's 'America' and his 'A Supermarket in California'. I loved the persona poems by Randall Jarrell. Notably I did not come to care much for John Berryman (who was a close friend of my father's in the Thirties). The influence of Bob Dylan (not just lyrics but voicing, timing, attitude) would be hard to overestimate.

PF: In 'Get it Again' "the waves roll out and the waves roll in" is an allusion to Weldon Kees. Does he have special meaning for you?

MH: Many years ago I was thrilled by Weldon Kees' poem 'Crime Club' and wanted to have written it. Also I love his 'Abstracts of Dissertations'. I haven't paid him much attention recently, but I'm glad you mention him, because I want to think about possible affinities between him and a good, strange poet I'm now reading, Kenneth Fearing, 1902-1961. Two very sour sarcastic men.

PF: Many of your poems ironize what we're supposed to feel – 'Hardened Mud', for example. Do you think we've become too sophisticated to put naive feeling into poems?

MH: 'Hardened Mud' might be seen as a nasty poem. But it's a kind of hostility that can feel necessary as a response to poseurs, writers whose emotions seem canned for sale. I feel a need to lash out like this, at times. But I think a poet can earn your trust, the way a person in life can; you see that this person really strives to be authentic, to dodge the convenient packages for Proper Feeling; and then, on occasion, that person can speak with direct "naked" emotion, under stress, and the effect is serious and powerful. Frank Bidart and Alan Shapiro and Cynthia Huntington (all friends of mine) are examples.

PF: Some traits in your work fit the postmodernist ticket: how do you feel about PM?

MH: "Postmodernism" has turned out to be a term almost as wildly flexible as "realism", hasn't it? If postmodernism means existentialism with humour, a sense that we can live in the fog of our confusion and the bog of our absurdity and still achieve innumerable acts of momentary bravado and bravery and sympathy, and even imagine some continuity between such acts, then I'm for it. If postmodernism means that we never have anything but irony, and the joke's always on anyone who tries to speak truth, and language is always only about its own failure, then I'm against it. The latter view, after all, is not only debilitating but ultimately boring.

PF: Your poetry ranges pretty omnivorously over low culture, and in 'Little Star' you make a claim for pop music – "this counts too alongside Beethoven" etc. Do you feel a crusading zeal about this?

MH: In the Eighties (my thirties) I did feel a bit of crusading zeal on behalf of pop music, but this was partly because I was allowing myself not to notice that the same battle was being fought by dozens and dozens of other poets. It was generational: we boomers were sliding out of our youth and we were damned if our cherished music of the Sixties and the late Fifties was going to be relegated to the attic for corny trivia. I feel protective toward the memory of particular songs (such as 'Little Star' by the Elegants) because their beauty seems so momentary and fragile and so bound-to-historical-setting (the doo-wop tradition, in the case of 'Little Star'), and such songs, such one-hit wonders, can seem ominous metaphors for one's own poems and the poems of one's friends. Meanwhile, in a more confident way I continue to admire Bob Dylan hugely; the word "great" fits him more decisively than it does any living poet. And I still consider the Beatles, the Rolling Stones, and the Kinks incredibly good in three different ways.

PF: You use music in your poems the way Larkin did – music as epiphany highlighting the long perspective. Do you read Larkin? Do you read English poetry?

MH: Yes, I've read and taught Larkin. I love 'Reference Back'. With Larkin you have to keep listening despite the crabbiness, as many critics have said. He seems to me to come amazingly close to greatness considering how little he wrote and how unsympathetic he could be. English poetry? After Larkin and Stevie Smith, I'm terribly vague. Geoffrey Hill has never seized me, though I've wanted to care about him because Christopher Ricks does and I respect Ricks very much. I sense a flim-flam element in Ted Hughes. Seamus Heaney is probably as excellent as several of my smartest friends think, though I've sometimes felt he was a bit too decent. Anyway, I need educating about contemporary English and Irish poetry; and I have a new friend in Fife who's trying to help me!

PF: Some people feel that it's time poetry in English was taken on its merits wherever it comes from but in practice people are still very parochial and tribal about poetry from their own patch. Do you think this is going to change?

MH: You might think it would break down in the electronic age, but I suspect the fearfulness of that info-barrage we were talking about tends to reinforce patchism. There is such a fear of disappearing in the flood. I have no doubt that certain British poets and certain Australian poets, for example, are much better than many of the American poets I read – but I haven't done well at finding them.

TWO POEMS BY MARK HALLIDAY

TRUMPET PLAYER, 1962

And when I get to Surf City I'll be shootin' the curls,
And checkin' out the parties for surfer girls.

When Jan and Dean recorded 'Surf City'
there must have been one guy –
I see this one trumpet player with his tie askew
or maybe he's wearing a loose tropical-foliage shirt
sitting on a metal chair waiting
for the session to reach the big chorus
where Jan and Dean exult
Two girls for every boy
                      and he's thinking
of his hundred nights on some buddy's hairy stainy sofa
and the way hot dogs and coffee make a mud misery
and the way one girl is far too much and besides
he hasn't had the one in fourteen months, wait,
it's fifteen now.
Surfing – what life actually lets guys ride boards
on waves? Is it all fiction? Is it a joke?
Jan and Dean act like it's a fine, good joke

whereas this trumpet player thinks it's actually shit,
if anybody asked him, a tidal wave of shit.
Nobody's asking.
The producer jiggles in his headphones. He wants more drums
right after *all you gotta do is just wink your eye!*

This producer is chubby and there is no chance,
my trumpet player thinks, that this chubhead gets
two swingin' honeys at any party ever and besides
on a given night a man only has one cock, or
am I wrong? And besides, you wake up wanting five aspirin
in an air lousy with lies, or half-lies.
And that's with only one girl.

But why am I so pissed here, he thinks,
when all these guys are hot for a hit?
Because I'm deep like Coltrane and they're all shallow,
right? Or because
I'm this smelly sour session man with a bent nose
and they're all hip to this fine fine joke?

The song is cooking, it's nearly in the can,
everybody has that hot-hit look
and my trumpet man has a thought: Sex
is not really it – what they're singing about –
they're singing about being here.
This dumb song is *it:*
this studio, this is the only Surf City,
here. And that's the great joke.

Okay, surf dicks, I am hip. But
there's gonna be pain in Kansas, he thinks,
lifting his horn and watching for the cue,
when they hear about Surf City and believe it.

ODD ITEM

It was like that time in Springfield
when the absence of a kiss predicted everything.
It was dark green with a dark blue patch.
It trembled in a rhythmic way like a picture of fear.
It reflected more light than you thought at first
like an apple on a Russian table.

It was much less explanatory than I expected.
It seemed to turn away and then glance back.
It was small, really, and you forgot it for quite a while.

It was like nothing I knew, but in a way
it was a lot like Alexander Pope.

It was like a TV comedian's salvo
except for the creepy twist near the end.
The pacing and the repetition were a little *off*
and we almost didn't even finish it.
There was something cold in how it just waited there.
Yet it caused me to think of coffee in Egypt.

In a way it wasn't quite as good as something
on page 129 of a novel you read three years ago.
Also one sensed that something awfully similar
might be found in the memoirs of some French writer
but smoother there, more combed, more *soigné*.

It was rather sweaty and loud
as if trying to be its own microphone.
You didn't want to be trapped in a tunnel with it.
Its gaze seemed to follow us like a dog's gaze
but then it sprang sideways
and whipped around the corner of Roxy Cinema.

We sort of watched it over our shoulders
like a possible malcontent at the far end of the bar.
Its raincoat bothered me. I circled the area
and returned from the south when the moon was right above it
and I was glad to be there again though I knew
it wasn't some huge thing.

It wasn't any great shakes; but
it wasn't someone else's shoe polish either.
We didn't pin it up over the bed,
neither did we chuck it with the nose-blown tissues.
It had its own margins. We left it
glowing in the dark and ducked back into our lives.

THE SONNET HISTORY

JOHN WHITWORTH
A SONNET HISTORY OF
ENGLISH POETRY 1900–1999

1.
From the plishy-plashy rushes, pitter-patter slips the otter,
Plippy-ploppy through the droppings see the nature poet putter.

2.
Something snickers in the woodshed, something stalks around the psyche,
Something darkling, disagreeable, malevolent and murky.

3.
It's *machinery*, not scenery, puts passion into verses:
Bash the bosses, trash the fascists and embrace the working classes.

4.
Luscious language soused in liquor with a whiff of myth and anguish –
Celtic fringes, Celtic binges (plus a whinge about the English).

5.
No kerfuffle, soft-shoe-shuffle, Mr B and Mr L
Tread a sad suburban measure down their primrose path to hell.

6.
Lay 'em low, the legless laddish, with the scything of a stanza –
Wendy, Sophie, Carol Ann and all that feminist bonanza!

7.
There's your formalist clinicians, post-post-Modern theoreticians,
Northern heathens, Martian persons, rhyming parsons and morticians. . .

Every Movement is a mirror, every pagan a believer,
Every poem is a moment, every moment is for ever.

REVIEWS

And So Farewell

RODDY LUMSDEN ON THE LAST RETROSPECTIVES TO MAKE THE MILLENNIAL CUT

The Nation's Favourite Twentieth Century Poems
Ed. Griff Rhys Jones
BBC £5.99
ISBN 0 563 55143 7

News That Stays News: The 20th Century in Poems
Ed. Simon Rae
Faber & Faber £9.99
ISBN 0 571 20060 5

NOTHING – NOT BOGUS champagne, not the eschatological sect, not even the overpaid bug basher – has proliferated in the past few years as rashly as the poetry anthology. Apparently, the millennium is the right time for us to make eyes at sonnets, performance pieces and short poems, poems on rivers, time, about parents and for life's moments of desperation. All this on top of the century round-ups which were to be expected. In a recent *Poetry Review*, Harry Clifton noted sagely that our clutch of wilful, often back-slapping anthologists offer us "approximations... which when taken together, may add up to some kind of general picture". But what of that arch-critic Mr Joe Public? Isn't it time the canny reader made his approximate stab?

With this National Poetry Day's song-lyric theme barring the possibility of another in the high-selling Nation's Favourite poetry series, the BBC have seen fit to release *Twentieth Century Poems*, the results of their 1996 poll. The assembled poems were seemingly deemed a potential poor seller at the time and should that prove to be true, the losses can surely be off-set against future volumes such as *The Nation's Favourite Cricketing Poems* which will undoubtedly follow.

In his jaunty introduction, Griff Rhys Jones maintains that the number of votes cast is always high enough "to pre-empt block claques and family conspiracies" (which doesn't quite explain the appearance of the madcap John Otway near the top of this year's song lyric poll). It is evidently also high enough to guarantee the appearance of the same "lowest denominator" factor which sends holiday novelty hits to the top of the "hit parade" and whichever party offers most free pizza into government.

To kick the book off, the BBC commissioned performance poet Benjamin Zephaniah to update Kipling's 'If' for the 1990s. What a splendid idea, Auntie! Zephaniah's "if"s are laudable, if barn-door predictable, but he stomps all over what is really quite a simple form in a manner sad to behold. When his signature poem 'Dis Poetry' turns up further in, between those of Hughes and Heaney (and if you feel over-familiar with 'The Thought Fox' and 'Digging', you might play the game of deciding which is the more portentously pompous), it is clear he has a problem with recognition of form – "I tek a Reggae Riddim and build me poetry", says BZ, but his rhythms, though they can be sparkling, are really a hybrid of 'The Lion and Albert' and the wonderful playground rhymes you can find collected in books by the Opie family.

It's no surprise to discover that many of the poems here have been on the school syllabus: the list of Larkin poems in George MacBeth's schoolbag staple *Poetry 1900–1965* is (albeit without 'This Be the Verse') more or less interchangeable with those favourites included here. Here we are encountering the force of Poetry Syndrome #17, wherein those lunks who loathe poetry at school, on becoming *d'un certain age*, suddenly discover a fondness for the lines which were drilled into them by cabbage-breathed English masters.

Also heartily represented are cats and doggerel, sometimes interbred. And, of course, death: lots of it, from Yeats' Irish airman to Hugh Grant stopping all the clocks to Mr Hegley's autumnal dog being "knoctober" (Oh, nurse, stitch my sides up!).

What's missing? Love, by my reckoning, and America. I found I had more than enough fingers to count the love poems in this book. The "men and women" section headed, "we have no hope of better / Happiness than this" contains two of Wendy Cope's witty, vinegary snipes and, for goodness sake, two poems about rape! Regarding Americans:

of the Anglos, Eliot is allowed some snippings from 'Little Gidding' and his *Erschrift*, 'The Waste Land', while Plath is represented only by the brilliant twin peaks of 'Daddy' and 'Lady Lazarus'. Thereafter, the American poetic century is frittered down to a mere five poems: Frost's ubiquitous 'Stopping by Woods...', three poems by those queens of the platitude, Maya Angelou and Alice Walker, and Cummings' candy-floss 'somewhere I have never travelled...' in which, if you wade through the knee-deep stickjaw, you will find the line, made famous by Woody Allen, "nobody, not even the rain, has such small hands".

You may recall that this poll was won by Jenny Joseph's 'Warning', of tea-towel fame. Ms Joseph has written in this publication that the poem has served her well over the years, yet word also has it that 'Warning' has so eclipsed her other, finer work that she wishes she had never written the thing. I have always understood it to be a tart and brilliant piece of satire which has, ironically, been lapped up by exactly the sort of woman it lampoons. Make your own mind up.

Beyond my hubris, I should note that this anthology isn't really aimed at the poetry maven and, as a stocking-filler for the occasional dabbler, it is rather good, especially when one considers its commendably sensible price-tag. Ultimately, it says less about the public's true taste in poetry than about the taste of those gullible enough to waste pennies on a poll phone call. Yet, as a reminder of evanescent poetic fads and as a catch-purse for jewels like 'The Whitsun Weddings', 'Not Waving But Drowning' and 'The Second Coming', the book succeeds, even if the century's motto, from the other side of the fence, may well appear to be, "What will survive of us is cats".

Wherever you stand in the debate on Faber's contemporary list in this time of change at the end of the Martian occupation, they still rule the anthology roost. Since great wodges of any anthology are culled from the Faber back-list, the situation is driven by economics. Their series of "hundred poem" collections is always exemplary, while Shapcott and Sweeney's *Emergency Kit* has been the decade's most essential poetry purchase. So Faber were always likely to find a lively project for that major domo among their anthologists, Simon Rae.

In *News That Stays News: The 20th Century in Poems*, Rae has selected a work to represent each year of the 1900s, from Hardy's war-inspired pessimism, in 1900's 'The Darkling Thrush', to John Heath-Stubbs commenting, ninety-nine years later, on the re-emergence of mythologised pessimism, though now we have flying saucers rather than flying songbirds to catch the updraught of our human panic.

One of the immediate charms of Rae's book is that he has limited each poet to one appearance and, in choosing poems which are of their time, or reflect the social or political *Zeitgeist*, he has frequently selected unfamiliar work. Removed of the responsibility of weighing poets against one another, Rae is free to concentrate on "poems" without the taint of the New Puritanism which would have us eradicate all personal context in our approach to reading poetry.

So here we find several poems not written by poets: occasional, emotional works which were largely inspired by "being there"; "there" for G. K. Menzies, writing in *Punch*, being the tax squeeze of 1905, for Phillip Whitfield, the corpse piles of Belsen. In any discussion of public poetry (as was the case with Andrew Motion's recent poem on the Ladbroke Grove train crash), there is always disagreement over whether the compassionate, but removed stance of a skilled practitioner is preferable to the passionate ineloquence of the observer. Rae's book offers fuel for all sides of the argument.

Inevitably, the focus is on the troubles of each passing decade, with war and its attendant politics taking centre stage. Here, in 1909, is John Davidson's rabid jingoistic cry of victory for the Empire in the arms race, the flag proclaiming "A future and a nobler world / where men and thoughts are free...". Glyn Maxwell's flawless 'Video Tale of a Patriot' reminds us in the '90s that such jingoism is still around, though thankfully more common on the letters pages of Teletext than among contemporary poets.

Though I hope that poets now accept their vocation as a nation's keenest cynics, rather than as flag-wavers, among my scarce qualms about this collection was a sense that the general tone (understandable in wartime, but it is sounded throughout, whether the subject is incursive politics or – perhaps too seldom – social change) was unstintingly negative. Either Rae feels (like Martyn Lewis's TV newsroom bosses) that good news is no news or poets have failed to respond to the incredible positive changes (medicine and technology, social welfare, the space race, the status of Western women) which have easily out-balanced the century's terrors. I found myself eager to be convinced that "the deep blue air" at the end of Larkin's ambiguous 'High Windows' (a perfect choice here for the adolescence of post-war Britain) was swimming with optimism after all, and not just another Larkinesque invocation of Death.

Readers will discover their own gems among the less-known work which Rae has unearthed, but I enjoyed MacDiarmid's anti-Christian bravado ("No Christian refuses to profit himself / from his brother's misfortune"), as invigorating in these days of smiley, cloak and dagger churches as it was refreshing in the '30s. Also, a poem composed by Craig Raine in a plane over Northern Ireland, "...Belfast below, a radio // with its back ripped off" represents a poet both literally and figuratively at a height. *News That Stays News* is certainly among the finest, least predictable and most painstakingly researched books you will find on the bulging anthology shelves and is highly recommended.

Only four poems appear in both books: 'The Second Coming' and 'Lady Lazarus' (both vigorous, visceral and uncommonly fine), Roger McGough's 'My Generation' (aka 'Let Me Die a Youngman's Death') and the eerie and moving 'Death of a Son' by Jon Silkin (whose own demise since the poll, unlike that of Hughes, the BBC has failed to note among the writers' dates). Whether, from these few poems, we can scry some truths about our present century as we squat on the brink of the next, I doubt. Let's make believe that the millennium will herald a brighter, affirmative time, full of poetry to temper our natural cynicism.

You can order these books POST-FREE from the PBS. See p.94 for details.

HELEN KITSON
THUNDERHEAD

At thirteen I told the lie
about the aspirin & the stomach pump;

at 16 I dangled the razor blade
but it cut no ice, nor skin.

It works for some girls, this gift
for holding others to ransom.

They are thunderheads, unpredictable,
with the force of thrown anvils.

I want my revenge, to be Thunderhead;
I want real pills, real black clouds

& hospital sheets. The real thing.
I want to be the girl who never fakes it.

THE CLASSIC FOUND POEM

SELECTED BY CATEGORICAL IMPERATIVE

THERE IS NO doubt about what is *the* found poem of the dying days of this millennium. On December 2nd the journal *Nature* announced the sequence of human chromosome 22. The remaining 22 chromosomes should be sequenced by 2003. We shall then a have a complete blueprint of a human being.

Chromosome 22 has 3.5 billion base pairs. It is a relatively small chromosome but it includes many interesting genes, including the schizophrenia suscepibility gene, that for spinocerebellar ataxia and the cat eye syndrome. The first 1000 bases in the sequence are as follows.

```
GATCTGATAAGTCCCAGGACTTCAGAAGAGCTGTGAGACCTTGGCCAAGTCACTTCCTCCTTCAGGAACATTGCAGTGGGCCTAAGTGCCTC-
CTCTCGGGACTGGTATGGGGACGGTCATGCAATCTGGACAACATTCACCTTTAAAAGTTTATTGATCTTTTGTGACATGCACGTGGGTTCCCAGTAG-
CAAGAAACTAAAGGGTCGCAGGCCGGTTTCTGCTAATTTCTTTAATTCCAAGACAGTCTCAAATATTTTCTTATTAACTTCCTGGAGGGAGGCTTATCA
TTCTCTCTTTTGGATGATTCTAAGTACCAGCTAAAATACAGCTATCATTCATTTCCTTGATTTGGGAGCCTAATTTCTTTAATTTAGTATGCAA-
GAAAACCAATTTGGAAATATCAACTGTTTTGGAAACCTTAGACCTAGGTCATCCTTAGTAAGATCTTCCCATTTATATAAATACTTGCAAGTAGTAGT-
GCCATAATTACCAAACATAAAGCCAACTGAGATGCCCAAAGGGGGCCACTCTCCTTGCTTTTCCTCCTTTTTAGAGGATTTATTTCCCATTTTTCTTAA
AAAGGAAGAACAAACTGTGCCCTAGGGTTTACTGTGTCAGAACAGAGTGTGCCGATTGTGGTCAGGACTCCATAGCATTTCACCATTGAGTTATTTC-
CGCCCCCTTACGTGTCTCTCTTCAGCGGTCTATTATCTCCAAGAGGGCATAAAACACTGAGTAAACAGCTCTTTTATATGTGTTTCCTGGATGAGC-
CTTCTTTTAATTAATTTTGTTAAGGGATTTCCTCTAGGGCCACTGCACGTCATGGGGAGTCACCCCCAGACACTCCCAATTGGCCCCTTGTCACCCA
GGGGCACATTTCAGCTATTTGTAAAACCTGAAATCACTAGAAAGGAATGTCTAGTGACTTGTGGGGGCCAAGGCCCTTGTTATGGGGATGAAG-
GCTCTTAGGTGGTAGCCCTCCAAGAGAATAGATGGTG
```

The Genetic Code

The instructions for life are contained in the sequences of bases that make up DNA and its sister molecule RNA. The DNA has the master set, and it uses different kinds of RNA as messengers to convey its instructions to the protein-making machinery.

Both DNA and RNA contain combinations of just four bases: Adenine (A), Guanine (G), Thymine (T), and Cytosine (C) in the case of DNA: in RNA the Thymine is replaced by the very similar Uracil (U).

Remembering that there are just 20 amino acids in proteins, the problem biologists faced in the 1960s was: how can 4 bases code for 20 proteins? If one base = one amino acid, only four different amino acids could be produced. If the bases were read in twos, there are 16 possible combinations of four bases read in twos – still not enough. If the bases are read in threes, there are 64 possible combinations. This is too many but it doesn't matter. After much ingenious experimental work it was conclusively proved by the end of the '60s that DNA does code in triplets to make proteins. Some amino acids have no less than 6 different codes that work for them, and three of the codes are not for proteins at all: they are stop signals, telling the machinery to end the chain at this point.

1st position	2nd position				3rd position
	U	C	A	G	
U	Phe	Ser	Tyr	Cys	U
	Phe	Ser	Tyr	Cys	C
	Leu	Ser	STOP	STOP	A
	Leu	Ser	STOP	Trp	G
C	Leu	Pro	His	Arg	U
	Leu	Pro	His	Arg	C
	Leu	Pro	Gln	Arg	A
	Leu	Pro	Gln	Arg	G
A	Ile	Thr	Asn	Ser	U
	Ile	Thr	Asn	Ser	C
	Ile	Thr	Lys	Arg	A
	Met	Thr	Lys	Arg	G
G	Val	Ala	Asp	Gly	U
	Val	Ala	Asp	Gly	C
	Val	Ala	Glu	Gly	A
	Val	Ala	Glu	Gly	G

All 64 possible triplets of the RNA bases that code for amino acids are shown in this table. Reading off the bases in each of the three positions gives the corresponding amino acid. For example, Adenosine in the first position, Uracil in the second and Guanine in the third (AUG) code for the amino acid Methionine (Met). It will be seen that for some amino acids there are several base codes: Serine, for example, has 6 different codes, ie there are 6 different ways of specifying Serine. This is an inevitable consequence of the fact that there are 64 triplets for only 20 amino acids.

A SECOND LOOK

An Anglo-Communist Poet

ANDY CROFT ON RANDALL SWINGLER

A FEW YEARS before he died, the poet Randall Swingler (1909–67) wrote a satirical memoir of the late 1920s, recalling the impact of the young Auden on would-be poets at Oxford:

When I first went up to Oxford, I had decided that I should find my place in the literary set. I imagined long walks with gentle sensitive companions beside the Thames to places with names like Bablock Hythe, and longer talks into the small hours in candle-lit rooms about Walter de la Mare and Robert Bridges and W. H. Davies, and about Beauty and Nature and perhaps – who knows ? – more daringly about Love. None of it quite worked out like that. In my time the literary world at Oxford, in fact the whole intellectual world, was dictatorially dominated by Mr Herryot Pendon. At no time and in no way was it possible to conceive of Mr Pendon as an undergraduate. Mr Pendon seemed to spend a great deal of his time during term in London, Berlin or Paris, from which he returned like a raiding force upon the University firing off names like Grosz, Cocteau, Marinetti. I gathered that all the writers I had ever admired, in fact all writers but a handful of whom I had never heard, were guilty of deliberately debasing language, perverting thought and feeling, and infecting the human race with homicidal mania, cancer and infantile paralysis. Shivering with horror and remorse, I looked at my own pitiful little imitations of early Yeats, Christina Rossetti and Browning, and realised the enormity of my corruption. This disgusting concept of Beauty which had fouled the relationship between the sexes, this revolting worship of Nature which had made the world a desert instead of a well-planned industrial area – how could I have fallen for it?

The joke is less on Auden (who had already left Oxford by Swingler's time) than on the narrator who falls, Spender-like, at the feet of the Master, renouncing English poetic tradition in the name of Modernity and politics. Few of Swingler's contemporaries were able to resist the example of Auden for long. Even Swingler, whose first collection *Poems* (1932) was an essentially Georgian sequence of love poems, fell briefly under the spell of the Audenesque in *Reconstruction* (1934) and *Difficult Morning* (1934). It is, however, worth remembering that English poetry contained other, potential lines of development in the late 1920s and early 1930s than the one that ran straight from *Oxford Poetry* to the offices of Faber and Faber. And as the subsequent career of Randall Swingler demonstrates, it was possible to address the urgent claims of Modernity in the middle decades of the century – politics, ideology, mass-society, war – without adopting the language of second-hand, second-generation Bloomsbury-Modernism, and without relinquishing the language of Beauty, Nature and Love. Modernist techniques were not the only way of responding to the challenges of the Modern world.

Like Auden, and like many of his class and generation, Swingler moved rapidly towards Marxism in the early 1930s (as the nephew and godson of the

Archbishop of Canterbury, Swingler's political trajectory was remarkable, even for those fervent times) and in 1934 he joined the British Communist Party. Unlike many of his (now) more famous contemporaries, however, he remained a Party member for more than twenty years, rapidly becoming the Party's best-known poet and cultural spokesman.

He was involved in the Workers Music Association and the Left Book Club, for whom he edited, with Alan Bush, the *Left Song Book*. He edited the magazine *Left Review*, where he published Nancy Cunard's *Authors Take Sides on the Spanish War*, and by the end of the 1930s was the literary editor of the *Daily Worker*. He was commissioned to write a new version of Peer Gynt for the Group Theatre (where he was assistant editor of the *Group Theatre Magazine*) and he wrote several plays for Unity Theatre, including the Mass Declamation *Spain*, the Munich-play *Crisis* and revues like *Sandbag Follies* and *Get Cracking*. In 1938 he launched his own radical paperback publishing company, Fore Publications, selling half a million of the Key Books series in the first twelve months. He and Alan Bush wrote the Living Newspaper *Peace and Prosperity* for the London Choral Union, a radically re-written production of Handel's *Belshazzar* for the London Co-operative Movement, and in 1939 they organised the Festival of Music and the People, including an Albert Hall pageant written by Swingler (starring Paul Robeson) and the premiere of Britten's *Ballad of Heroes* (for which Swingler and Auden wrote the libretto).

During the War he served as a Corporal with the Eighth Army in North Africa and Italy; he was involved in both the Anzio and the Salerno landings, and was awarded the Military Medal for bravery. After the war, he edited the radical Fitzrovian magazines *Our Time*, *Arena* and *Circus*. He left the Communist Party in 1956, and joined the editorial board of the *New Reasoner*.

For all that he was publicly identified for so long with the political campaigns and causes of the Communist Party, however, Swingler's poetry remained rooted in the traditional landscapes of Nature, Beauty and Love, a combination which one critic called "Anglo-Communism". His models were Bridges and Thomas rather than Auden or Eliot, and his subject was not the *History of the CPSU (B)* but the English countryside. Consider, for example, his most widely anthologised poem,

'Acres of Power':

Acres of power within me lie,
Charted fields of wheat and rye
And behind them, charted, too,
Brooding woods of beech and yew.
Beyond them stretch, uncharted yet,
Marsh and mountain, dark and wet,
Whence sometimes in my dreams and ease
Strange birds appear among the trees.

The fields of corn are action's fruit,
Gripping the earth with puny root,
Their surface pattern neatly planned
Upon the chaos of my land.
Against the ruminating wood
They set a fence, but to no good;
The shadow and the sap of mind
Still weighs the harvest of my hand.

And the wild marshes and the hills
Shut out by the imposing will
Yet hurl their livid storms across
To smash the fence and flood the fosse
And all his dictates and his laws
Cannot restrain the surging force
For the whole land is my power still,
Divided, fenced, but no less real.

And one man only mourning goes
By day through the stiff planted rows
By night through the tangled wood, to gaze
On the vast, savage wilderness.
The born surveyor, he that would
Turn the whole acreage to good,
Subject to one coherent plan
Dispensing the whole power of man.

But he between the fences dour,
This organiser of my power,
By rigid area is confined
That severs impulse, hand and mind.
For he is only paid to see
That the fields grow obediently
And that the woods do not encroach
Nor the trees part to show the marsh.

For if the power that lavish there
Breaks into a sterile air,
Were planned and planted, fibre and juice,
And all my earth enlaced with use
Then evil for his ruler's case

Whom to maintain in idleness
My fields of power are bought and sold
And all their goodness changed for gold.

Thus the land that is my life
Divided, ruled, and held in fief,
All the power it could produce
He cannot sell, but I could use.
And my surveyor, grim and harsh,
In secret now reclaims the marsh
That cultivated acres there
May bear a fruit for all to share.

When Swingler collected his 1930s verse, together with poems he had written in Africa and Italy, in *The Years of Anger* (1946) he did not include any of his public, occasional, propagandist verse (the Britten song 'Advance Democracy', for example, his chorale finale for Bush's Piano Concerto, the many poems he had written about the war in Spain). Instead, he published a selection of personal, lyric poems charting the inner development "of someone implicated, as we all were in our varying degrees of consciousness, in the stress of those years". The result was an extraordinary and beautiful collection of poems about love and loss and fear and hope, written "in the silence while we wait for the guns to go off", reconstructing the emotional, intellectual and natural landscapes of pre-war England.

The Years of Anger should have sealed Swingler's reputation as an unflinching witness to his time and generation, a link between the romantic Communism of the early 1930s and the anti-Fascist victory of 1945, a traditional English lyric poet in the Modern world. Unfortunately, it was ignored by Communist press and literary London alike. The Manichean orthodoxies of the Cold War did not understand such a highly personalised lyrical sensibility that was both traditional in form and radical in politics. Swingler was attacked as a "bohemian" and an "aesthete" inside the Communist Party, publicly denounced by Orwell and witch-hunted at the BBC. There was no room in Cold War London for this kind of poetry or for this kind of poet. Mr Herryot Pendon and his disciples – all paid-up *anti*-communists by now – had won, and English poetry had lost one of its most distinctive and radical voices.

Trent Editions are publishing *The Selected Poems of Randall Swingler*, edited by Andy Croft, and Shoestring Press are publishing Andy Croft's *Letter to Randall Swingler* later this year.

COLETTE BRYCE
GRIFFON

We queue at the valley's screened enclosure,
take our places, pay a price, a thousand pesetas
apiece for this; for you, a mash of blood and flesh,
a metal pail, a tethered foot, a note on natural habitat,
a roaring anger in your gut that keeps you lunging
from your rope, upward, to your element.

A whistle shrieks
and you release your vast scaffolding of wings,
perform a weighted, awkward flight, a single beat
from A to B, then low across our cowered heads
to A. You earn your piece of meat, regard us
with an ancient eye. Up there, a pencilled sketch
of peaks, eternity of sky, a far cry.

IAN PARKS
THE DOUBLE MAN

1
In my dream there had been civil wars;
some pestilence was ravaging the land.
We'd fled from northern cities still ablaze
where fall-out shelters slanted to the earth

and met again by chance on a dark road
among ten-thousand refugees. I knew
him by the way he cupped his hand
around the sharp-drawn instant

of a cigarette to be the spokesman
of the border and the group, boyish
in his drab, ill-fitting suit, who flicked
his 'thirties crop back from his eyes,

peered at me sideways, then began.
The landscape that I wrote about has changed;
the ruined workings are still there
but now more ruinous. A dream

of dereliction meets you everywhere:
cooling towers crumble and collapse,
furnaces sift black chambers of cold ash;
pit-heads have fallen into disrepair.

Even the airman poised above it all
sees only what he wants to see –
bare coastlines beaten by harsh tides
and suburbs spread below him on the plain.

The stranger on this island now turns back,
spares only the slightest of glances
for the fells and passes he came through.
He is no lover of these broken shires

or the land of farms that has had its day.
When all is said and done our time is short.
You are still young; you must take your chances
with the rest and if you fail

you fail. My advice is this:
listen to the rhythms of your heart
and nothing else; treat what you do
as some long complex game

then set about to shatter every rule.
Love and Death, these two writ large
still constitute the common theme;
take from them what you need and forget

about the rest. The prophet's day is over now –
the poet and the hero on the lawn
but all the questions of the past remain.
Great country houses open their doors

to Sunday morning visitors,
while in the suburbs disaffected wives
turn their deft hands to fresh accomplishments:
spinning, weaving, poetry; arranging

flowers in the Anglo-Norman crypt.
A folly marks the spot where lovers wept.
Concrete pill-boxes keep a narrow-slitted watch
on coastlines where no enemy will tread.

When darkness comes upon the counties of your mind,
do you sleep easy in your bed?
As for myself, I said to him,
I work for neither wages nor success.

The urgency of here and now
is with me all my waking hours
and that Old Pretender – History
concerns me less and less.

I turned to you for an answer
but found only the answer of your flight
which is no answer in the end. One learns
from one's experience but never fast enough.

Post-war and post-imperial,
a generation with its own concerns

*at the end of a bad century
what is there left to say?*

*What promises are left for us to keep?
He shrugged his shoulders and looked away,
pointing to the distance aimlessly.
I fell into an instant sleep.*

2
When I woke again the scene had changed:
a station platform's raftered curve
arched high above us where we stood.
He stooped towards me, older now,

his accent pointed, half-American;
the smell of death still clinging to his clothes.
You see how changed I am, he said to me.
There's one bare hour of darkness left

*before I have to leave. Listen to what I say.
This is the city where I was born,
where the Ouse still flows
its dark protracted course*

*past palaces and factories alike.
On August evenings tourists going home
cram ornamental bridges with their cars.
It wasn't always so. You came*

*in search of my birthplace once
and went home disappointed
by the meagre metal plaque.
And on park benches lovers sit in pairs,*

*their talk profuse as pollen on the breeze.
In hotel rooms the bright lights dance
with love and love's experience.
We test our living in cities like this*

*with its wide mellow walls
and monumental spires. If I'd stayed
to walk these streets, what sort of poet
would I have been? One given*

to false securities I'd guess.
What it comes down to in the end
is the love of a handful of people.
Look at those two standing at the rail:

the rain has seared their eyes, their open mouths,
and still they stand and kiss
under the station porticoes.
It doesn't matter that by their journey's end

love might have turned to bland indifference.
It is the moment – composite, secure –
insinuates itself into your lines.
Forget the forlorn traffic of this place;

commuters running with their daily weight
against the pressures of their day.
Avoid the flattery of careless eyes
and voices demanding their own terms.

Steer clear of the honest, seeming-open face
and the dangerous linking of arms.
There is only this to say:
consider your father and your son

and how, in everything that's done
there is a loving and more loving one.
He finished and the intercom crackled loud,
its destinations overscored

by the sudden onrush of a train.
Distracted by its hollow sound
I turned to see bright windows flashing past
into the dark, and when I looked again

he'd gone without a gesture or a word,
shambling off towards the barrier.
Head down, alone, anonymous at last
he disappeared into the milling crowd.

SARAH WARDLE
SOCRATES TO DESCARTES

When on earth, you and I weren't sure of much,
only things, like God and Justice, one can't touch.
Concepts had to start with an upper case
before we would let them past second base.
But the old days were good: you by your fire,
glass in hand, me with ouzo and a lyre,
dancing girls on a Platonic table,
and young lads. Of what weren't we capable?

You see it's the physical stuff I miss.
Since the hemlock, I've put emphasis
on experience, not universals,
on live performance, not dress rehearsals.
In the heavens we spin through thought and space,
but want feet on the ground, a heart, a face.
Reduced to brains in a galactic vat,
we'd trade Ideas to get our bodies back.

PHILIP GROSS
TALES OF THE FOREST

They say the real Bluebeard's Castle
is just up the road from here
    but then so do twenty other villages
    between the airport and the border zone.

A coach leaves on the hour.
We could go, we two, among the dozens.
    There's a buffet thrown in, braised
    hearts and strawberries and the local brew.

It would mean getting out of our bed
in the Honeymoon Suite: a curt
    start after breakfast and the guide
    with matching lipstick, clipboard, scarlet blazer

wants us organised in ethnic groups;
she can swivel from language to language,
    click, click. All that puts me off
    is that one must be English,

not the patter (like rain moving in
in the night as we wake to taste each other
    one more time) of a language
    we don't have to understand. No,

let's drift to the dining room,
asking for breakfast at midday,
    stay late in the bar, past
    some notion of bedtime, just to tease,

touching toes beneath the table
as we let Mister Been-here-before
    buttonhole us with his tale –
    of a friend of a friend, in a hire car,

driving through the forest when a boar,
a real wild one, ran straight out; he swerved
    but caught the beast a cruncher –
    like an upholstered boulder, he said –

and he spun off in the ditch,
his radiator hissing, the whole wing
    crumpled in; the boar staggered,
then ran on, and three piglets came after,

straight over, back into the underbrush,
leaving just the hiss of steam
    and his heart, and a dim sense
    none of this had ever been.

JOHN KINSELLA
MUSHROOMING

"Out there..." out there where sheep dung
collates and top-dressed soil exudes
decomposing nitrogen, where under-rings
filigree networks of sensitivity
uneasy as roundup drifts from firebreaks
and first rains stimulate filaments;
where THE LAND does its urge thing,
conscious of literary precedent,
all that nudge and mystery
and primal aching: *clair de lune*,
the push-button radio astronomy
with calling occupants precision
in the blur of the between-seasons
evening – and yes, I'm afraid they DO believe it;
and yes, pink and grey and loud despite
a chill setting in: you know what *we've*
been reading. So, mushrooms
stem-severed and bagged, gills riddled
with field krill, rise to the less-pressured
waters, that is, out of the light-starved
trenches, rotting in sacks already bruised.
The disc plough wastes no time
before cutting in, breaking systems
of mycelium, night growth and industry.
Decay feeds and is bled: the freelancing
narratology of marketing boards.

TWO POEMS BY LAWRENCE SAIL
THE ADDICTION

All this came late, as seemed to befit a house
with no father, where taboos had a low threshold –
you could make do with a sniff at an empty beer-bottle,
a lick of its black nubbed stopper; or with a quick
glimpse of the pub when the frosted door swung open,
the waft of talk and smoke yeastily there
and gone again. Once, a bottle of rum
with a top you flipped up, and the strange smell of dunder.

The litany of brands could well have been
a sufficient lure – Craven 'A', Abdullah,
Woodbines, Capstan Full Strength, Senior Service,
Player's Navy Cut, Du Maurier, Three Castles,
Gold Flake, Gitanes, Gold Leaf, even the absurd
exotic Balkan Sobranies with their gold-tipped black,
and the ones in soft packs closed with a paper seal:
Lucky Strike, Disques Bleus, Camels, Chesterfield.

Then, the procedures: the opening of the little drawer,
the whoosh, soft as satin, when you whisked away
the gold or silver foil, to expose them ranged
in perfect order, close and regular
as boxed eggs. Or, breaking the seal,
you gave that one authoritative tap
which brought out two or three just so far,
stacked like organ pipes, ready to offer.

Think what it did for timing and expression:
the flick of fire, the head inclined and then
tossed back, the lips and cheeks closed in on
the searing circle, the arc of the hand, the cool
considered exhalation and the look
that went with it. Thus could entire systems
be stubbed out, complex disputations won,
ennui be dramatised, or an affair begun.

It took another twenty years to learn
that real addiction might be something else –
the world returning, hyper-real enough

to drag your eyes from their sockets, and the size
of every leaf outsize, each object swollen
with its own savour and abundance. Even to enjoy,
when it was safe, the whiff of cedar and, slightly,
of caporal in the box with no cigarettes.

KADDISH

This is a song of a song gone missing
in which children were fearless and ran
straight for the eye of the wobbly camera,
put out their tongues and waved their hands.

This is also the raw edge of music
the black intervals' virtual dissonance
in which the violin almost remembers
how once it played for weddings and dances.

In the missing song, grown-ups were kind
and parents there to run into, always –
mother in the dress that smelt of safety,
father taking pictures of family holidays.

Here is the way back never to be taken
to the peaceable kingdom of praise and thanks
where all puffs of gunsmoke simply exploded
into lightsome feathers, and all bullets were blanks.

This is a song of a song gone missing,
with words simple as pebbles, inferring
a sense that the mind can no longer admit
or the heart still quite unlearn.

THE REVIEW PAGES

The Restless Past

BERNARD O'DONOGHUE ON HEANEY AND HUGHES

SEAMUS HEANEY

Beowulf
Faber & Faber £14.99
ISBN 0 571 201 13 x

TED HUGHES

The Oresteia
Faber & Faber £7.99
ISBN 0 571 17996 7

SINCE ELIOT IDENTIFIED in Joyce a capacity which he called "the mythic imagination", the use of myths has been a particularly favoured recourse for writers in the attempt to express authoritative meaning. The most potent source of the mythic is past literature: so far past that it does not seem to be part of the same continuum covered by such terms as "English Literature". This turning to myth was not new in the twentieth century of course; Romantic poetry, from Keats's Gothic to Tennyson's 'Ulysses' and 'Tithonus', went to the myths of the past to cope with the expressive demands of the great subjects – love and life and justice and, above all, death. But Eliot was observing something different from nineteenth-century practice; then the fundamental energy in poetry was narrative and the stories were translated directly into modern terms; for example when Dante's Ulysses in Tennyson's version says "'Tis not too late to seek a newer world", he is giving expression to a current ideal of late Empire. By contrast the connexion between Leopold Bloom and Odysseus (who is also Ulysses of course) is much looser. Often the mythic parallel for modernist writers is oppositional rather than confirming.

The simultaneous appearance of these two translations, by the duumvirate that has dominated English poetry on this side of the Atlantic for twenty years, raises again the question of the use of myth. George Steiner in *Antigones* argues that the issues in Greek literature have remained the fundamental ethical-political questions since their own time, offering a kind of language of high emotion, and crucially so for our era (he is thinking, amongst other things, of the Holocaust). Similarly, Seamus Heaney said that when he encountered in medieval Irish the story about Sweeney the displaced Ulster poet, he thought "there's something here for me". These two views offer interesting similarities and contrasts; the Steiner position is a new, existentialist one, different from earlier uses of myths for their topicality: nobody nowadays will claim comparability with the dilemmas faced by Antigone or Oedipus or Orestes. These legendary Greek figures are invoked as the transcendent instance of the emotion they express – horror, tragedy, grim revenge – and thus to purge the lesser, everyday experiences of the same feelings. In the Heaney case there is a direct resemblance between the defeated and banished Sweeney travelling transformed over the whole of Ireland and the poet's own leaving Ulster for the South of Ireland. Equally directly, Yeats in *The King's Threshold* invokes Fergus, the king who abandons his throne in order to be a poet, and Seanachan – the poet who starves himself to death on the steps of King Guaire's palace as a protest against the public slighting of poetry – in order to make his case for the prominence of Art in his concept of a new, ideal Ireland. Yeats's position is, at least to some extent, *like* that of Fergus and Seanchan, as Heaney's is like Sweeney's. The distinction between these two uses of myth is recognizable as another case of "The Battle of the Books", the classical Ancients versus the vernacular Moderns.

The point I am making somewhat crudely is that different mythic systems are used for different purposes by modern poets and we have to bear in mind the implications of each. This has been particularly prominent in the major poets of Northern Ireland over the past forty years. A striking division among those poets is whether they turn to Irish or

Classical myths (Heaney has repeatedly turned to both); recourse to the classics represents a claim for universality, while the use of a post-classical myth claims topicality. It is important to make this distinction clear to avoid loading the dice too heavily in favour of the ancients, given the weight of the term "Classical" itself.

So what might a poet be thought to be buying into by translating the modern-era *Beowulf* and Aeschylus, the most classical of all tragedians, in the 1990s? There is an immediate paradox here which Heaney raises in his introduction: although the Old English of *Beowulf* is the antecedent of our language and Aeschylus's Greek was recorded in a foreign script and language two-and-a-half millennia ago, the characters and themes of the *Oresteia* are more familiar to us. As Heaney puts it "Achilles rings a bell but not Scyld Scefing". This is like Steiner's claim that Greek tragedy does not require topical justification; but what does the opaque and unfamiliar *Beowulf* offer as a modern myth? These two new versions make it easier to gauge Heaney's intentions than Hughes's because *Beowulf* is preceded by a 22-page introduction in which Heaney spells out what drew him to the poem; Hughes's black-liveried *Oresteia* is sternly free of any apparatus that might have suggested the plays' bearing on modern times, beyond the information that the publication coincides with a National Theatre production directed by Katie Mitchell. This somewhat veiled procedure is typical of Hughes, whose late blossoming (reblossoming might be more accurate) has produced a series of surprises, not least in the wonderful plainstyle translations in *Tales from Ovid*. His *Oresteia* is decidedly Hughesian in the way the wiry vernacular springs to life at moments of violence (rather than tension), particularly those voiced by women – by Clytemnestra, or the Furies as Chorus in *Eumenides*. A language which is never less than eloquent and is often colloquial then develops a *Crow*-like intensity:

> A man in his splendour
> Is like the sun.
> But when the blood from someone he has killed
> Spills into his conscience
> He sinks into the black clouds of our [the Furies']
>   tatters.
> Then the living blood that beats in the head
> Is the drum of vengeance.

In view of the tragic fact that this *Oresteia* is revenant-poetry by Hughes – like his Alcestis a voice from the grave – it is striking how reminiscent of 'Under Ben Bulben' this "man" is, both in splendour and in violence. By contrast with this fierce late-Yeats poetry, some of the more celebrated set pieces of these most celebrated of all plays are dealt with in a language of dramatic clarity rather than rhetorical power. It is revealing, for example, to contrast Hughes's weatherworn watchman at the opening of *Agamemnon* with the extraordinarily powerful creation Heaney makes of him in 'Mycenae Lookout' in *The Spirit Level*. Heaney seizes on Aeschylus's graphic "But for the rest I am silent; a great ox stands / upon my tongue" (in Lloyd-Jones's close translation) for his epigraph to the poem; Hughes omits the ox, saying rather slangily

> And then – what follows,
> Better not think about it...
> Those who know too much, as I do, about this
>   house,
> Let their tongue lie still – squashed flat.

The women's chorus at the end of *Choephori* are also oddly prosaic:

> Can the poor, scorched brains of Orestes
> Figure out all the factors? Can he solve
> The arithmetic of the unfinished
> That shunts this curse from one generation to the next?

For all its power and clarity on the stage, often the plainstyle which Hughes used so hauntingly in *Birthday Letters* reads rather reductively here. In the end, although we can begin to understand in a general way why Hughes was working with Euripides's *Alcestis* – the "late-espoused saint" – in the months before his death, the overall direction of his Aeschylus is harder to intuit. It is of course a dilemma that Hughes himself has discussed with great urgency in 'Myths, Metres, Rhythms': the difficulty of steering a consistent course between the whole language and the demands of modern expression. He is at his most powerful in the determinism of *Eumenides*, as Athene addresses (and solves) the problem of the seemingly implacable Furies: "if their case fails, what happens to their anger?". Strangely though, the closing palliation of them, which in Aeschylus seems still founded in fearful euphemism, manages to suggest peaceful resolution in Hughes's ending:

So God and fate, in a divine marriage,
Are made one in the flesh
Of all our people –
And the voice of their shout is single and holy.

This *is* Hughes's own Aeschylus, and one that makes peace with the world. I am not sure that it will become the standard reader's version of Aeschylus in English, but it will certainly have a distinguished place both in the Theatre repertoire and in the Hughes canon.

Heaney's serendipity in turning to *Agamemnon* for 'Mycenae Lookout' was more readily intelligible in its return to the issues of North, especially the question of non-affiliation in civil war through the power of his exploited Cassandra and her introduction through horrific self-contradiction:

No such thing
as innocent
bystanding.

Her soiled vest,
her little breasts:

surely this *is* innocent bystanding. But why is Heaney translating *Beowulf* – an ancient Germanic semi-legendary assemblage of fairy-story monsters and pseudo-history? Why has he felt this to be a tract for the times? This remains not entirely clear even at the end of his exuberant and compelling introduction. Connexions are made: "The Geat woman who cries out in dread as the flames consume the body of her dead lord could come straight from a late-twentieth-century news report, from Rwanda or Kosovo; her keen is a nightmare glimpse into the minds of people who have survived traumatic, even monstrous events and who are now being exposed to a comfortless future". We note the opportunist seizing on the "monstrous" as a link: the Heaney skill felicitously dubbed recently by Helen Vendler as his "etymological tuning-fork". He describes the *Beowulf* world brilliantly as "one with no very clear map-sense of the world, more an apprehension of menaced borders". Overall the introduction presents as motivation a kind of debt of honour: Heaney's expression of fealty to the English poetic tradition at its root. From his student-days he recalls Old English poetic language as the source of the Hopkins language that most influenced him (celebrated in Heaney's great essay 'The fire i'th'flint'. And there are more particularly Heaneyesque themes; the poem's deterministic monsters, Grendel and the dragon, dark creatures of evil whose actions have been laid down since the time of Cain, are readily accommodated within Heaney's northern Bog-myths. Heaney significantly calls the dragon "more *wyrd* (Fate) than *wyrm* (serpent)". But the particular aptnesses are not the point; Heaney ends his introduction with the words of his own poem 'The Settle Bed', to suggest the relentless fatalistic driving forward through the generations that he finds in *Beowulf* and which characterizes his version: "willable forward / again and again and again".

The power and eloquence of Heaney's version could be illustrated from almost anywhere in his *Beowulf* which shows the benefit of the careful ten years spent on it. Here is the end of one of the poem's great set-pieces, 'The Lay of the Last Retainer', so beloved in the nineteenth century:

No trembling harp,
no tuned timber, no tumbling hawk
swerving through the hall, no swift horse
pawing the courtyard.

This could be nothing but Old English elegy; but it could be nobody but Heaney either. The translation was done in response to an invitation from the Norton Anthologists, and Heaney has met their demand magnificently. I think this will become the Reader's *Beowulf* for the foreseeable future.

In the end the fundamental difference is between the two poets' inclinations rather than between the works or the literary cultures turned to. Heaney is a co-opter; Hughes is warier, keeping his distance and allowing general congruences to settle or be inferred. In addition Heaney is a public poet; if you don't see why he writes about Cassandra or the social healing of the mead-hall in *Beowulf*, you miss the point of the work. We may feel tempted to supply modern correspondences for Hughes's Furies or Alcestis or Clytemnestra, but on the whole it seems better not to. Certainly nothing is lost by not making such links. This distinction is borne out by the respective languages of the two poets. Heaney, in a two-way co-option, reserves the right to introduce Ulsterisms into his versions which are hardly less foreign to Old English than they are to Greek: "bawn", "brehon", "graith", "kesh" (the Norton editors, he tells us, drew the line at "gilly") in *Beowulf* recalling the local language of Philoctetes in *The Cure at Troy*. Modernizing of syntax in

Heaney is done in an Ulster accent: "so ought a kinsman act" (*Beowulf*); "Let me tell you, son, the way they deserted me" (*The Cure at Troy*). Hughes's modernizations are into a colloquial form of modern English: "I'm sick of the heavens, sick of the darkness". The most remarkable significance of these two books though is in showing how the recent domination of English poetry by this powerful and friendly pairing has not been lessened by Hughes's death.

You can order these book POST-FREE from the PBS. See p.94 for details.

Trouble and Strife

by Carol Rumens

CAROL ANN DUFFY

The World's Wife

Picador, £10
ISBN 0 330 37221 1

"IT IS THANKS to myth that we believe that woman must be either angel or monster", or so Alicia Ostrika claimed in her study of American women's poetry, *Stealing the Language* (The Women's Press, 1987). Perhaps, though, the belief came first and the myth grew out of that? Chicken-and-egg riddles aside, feminist myth-revision is a major theme of twentieth-century writing: Ostrika traces it back to the nineteenth century when "women used heroines like Sappho and Eve as a cover for writing erotic verse and heroines like Medea and Ariadne for the forbidden theme of women's rage". In the nineteen-sixties and seventies the genre was newly flourishing in the hands of such poets as Muriel Rukeyser, Anne Sexton, Sylvia Plath, Sandra Gilbert, Margaret Atwood and others. In England, too, poets have been attracted to the genre, though the most spectacular contribution, perhaps, was a work of prose fiction, Angela Carter's 1979 collection of richly re-imagined fairy-tales, *The Bloody Chamber*. The risk inherent in the genre is that of formulaic writing that cannot escape the stereotypes and boundaries imposed by the original, and simply reverses them in the heroine's favour. But it is also a source of enormous opportunity. Myth-making permits the big voice, the self-dramatisation, that even now may seem off-limits to poets in general and women poets in particular. It's significant, surely, that a writer as vocally confident and achieved as Carol Ann Duffy should, on the evidence of the new collection, nevertheless have found her range extended by the medium.

The World's Wife draws on a variety of sources – Greek myths, fairy tales, the Bible and, occasionally, the tabloid press. Few of the poems fail to send tingling subtle nerve-ends to the present: they are better than much of the earlier work in the genre at conveying the impression that the world's wives and husbands, far from being locked in the fabulous or folksy are alive and kicking. A few are fairly routine tales of female exasperation, extended husband-jokes or tirades that, while they may break a taboo for the imaginary speaker, rouse no more than a frisson of complicity in the contemporary reader. Mood and diction may become almost interchangeable when Mrs Sisyphus, Mrs Aesop and Mrs Icarus cast scornful eyes on their partners, though Mrs Sisyphus hammers home her disapproval with particular force – the usual short lines plus a battering-ram of rhyme:

> Think of the perks, he says.
> What use is a perk, I shriek,
> when you haven't the time to pop open a cork
> or go for so much as a walk in the park?
> He's a dork.
> Folk flock from miles around just to gawk.
> They think it's a quirk,
> a bit of a lark.
> A load of old bollocks is nearer the mark.

These wives are entering poetry for the first time, and a certain excitement for reader and writer is connected to that: others step out of a strong tradition of revisionist writing (male and female) and invite comparisons. Perhaps Duffy was right to go for a slickly comic, hard-girl Euridice, inevitably a less mysterious creation than the woman Rilke so memorably brings to ghostly life in his triptych. Duffy's Euridice, happily dead, secures her release from the threatened resurrection by tricking her dreadful husband into turning round: "Orpheus, your poem's a masterpiece. / I'd love to hear it again". This monologue, like several others, delib-

REVIEWS

erately includes the woman reader ("Girls, I was dead and down", etc.) inviting us into collusion. It is not simply that the vitality of the language is guaranteed by direct speech but that communal energies are also being drawn on. Some of the poems that spread a little thinly on the page would no doubt be sure-fire in performance.

But, for the reader, the more complex the poem's narrative, diction and characterisation, the better. Slang expressions like "stuff that", "When it comes to the crunch", "load of bollocks", etc. take on a new force when, by virtue of the surrounding linguistic company, they demand to be read for their residual metaphor and not just their colloquial exuberance. Like Sylvia Plath, Duffy enjoys splicing literary and vernacular idioms. Generally, the longer line and biggish-stanza construction best suit her purposes. There are poems here that seem to occupy a sphere where revisionist mythmaking is only a small part of the total engagement: new myths, with deeply buried personal roots, are being forged, strange and raw and haunting. 'Thetis', 'Mrs Midas', 'Queen Herod', 'Medusa', 'The Kray Sisters' are resonant and large-scale: of the smaller pieces, 'Anne Hathaway', is a gem, a chastely ecstatic love-poem whose form, the Shakespearean sonnet, is part of its shy homage. Not all the revisions are limited to debunking, to adjusting down. 'Pilate's Wife', somewhat bypassing Pilate, gives us an extraordinary image of Christ, crucified between the sexual ("His eyes were eyes to die for") and the sacred ("Was he God? Of course not. Pilate believed he was"). The narrator here seems not quite reliable despite her apparent candour and pragmatism, but that tremor makes the poem extraordinary. An even less reliable narrator in 'The Devil's Wife' seems to be trying to make sense of the woman as criminal: she is a Rose West or Myra Hindley figure, given a voice but only fitfully able to articulate the horror she knows she has unleashed :"But what did I do to us all, to myself / When I was the devil's wife?"

The World's Wife begins with a poem that is really a parable about the woman poet's artistic coming-of-age, a version of the Little Red-Cap story in which the heroine first admires and learns from the male-poet-wolf, then goes on to discover (as he has forgotten) that "Words, words were truly alive in the head, / warm, beating, frantic, winged; music and blood". The creation of living words exacts a price: it involves violence and may be a particularly tough lesson for the woman artist, though it seems romantically easy here: "I took an axe to a salmon / to see how it leapt. I took an axe to the wolf". If this is an important collection, breaking new ground in spite of its indebtedness to feminist tradition, the reason lies in the fact that while most of its heroines are feisty, courageous, sexy, self-forging individuals, there is no false innocence, no refusal of the full human possibility, including evil. Not all the victories are foregone conclusions: not all the conclusions are victories (see 'Medusa'). There are poems here still at the re-balancing stage of revisionism but many others use the re-balanced world as their starting-point, and recognise that here, too (luckily for poetry), no-one is perfect.

You can order this book POST-FREE from the PBS at £10. See p.94 for details.

Home Win

by Ian McMillan

ROGER MCGOUGH
The Way Things Are
Viking £9.99
ISBN 0 670 88655 6

ME REVIEWING A book by Roger McGough is like me writing a report on a Barnsley match; I can't find any fault, even if it's a boring nil-nil draw. This certainly isn't a nil-nil draw, though: it's a decisive home win with some brilliant passages of play, some great finishing, and the kind of consistency that only comes with experience.

The home win idea really fits because these days a lot of McGough's work is centred on home and family and the realities of closeness and love. The title poem is a fugue of odd shiny truths from a father to a son: "No, old people do not walk slowly / because they have plenty of time, / Gardening books when buried will not flower. / Though lightly worn, a crown may leave a scar, / I am your father and this is the way things are". This stanza has a number of McGough's trademarks: the craft worn as lightly as the crown, the jokes that are something more, the underlying heartache, the acute sense (found even in poems from all those years ago) of the way time slips away. The other thing that McGough is very good at is taking ordinary phrases, overheard snippets of tired old sentence-shards and giving them new life. In 'Half-Term' he (to use a McGoughish idea) does things by halves: "Half-term holiday, family away / Half-wanting to go, half-wanting to stay / stay in bed for half the day. // Half-read, half-listen to the radio, / half-think things through. Get up, / half-dressed, half-wonder what to do". In 'An Ordinary Poetry Reading' he worries at that idea, no doubt muttered in McGough's direction at a gig somewhere, of An Ordinary Poetry Reading: "Tonight will be an ordinary poetry reading, / A run of the mill kind of affair! Nothing that will offend or challenge / No language as far as I'm aware. // The poets are thoroughly decent / all vetted by our committee / We had hoped Wendy Cope might appear / but she's tied up more's the pity". 'Balloon Fight' is a perfect example of the genre, and should teach us to keep out ears open all the time; the epigraph is from the *Today* programme ("This morning, the American, Steve Fossett, ended his round-the-world balloon fight... I'm sorry, balloon flight... in northern India") and the poem plays with that idea like a child folding and tearing paper to make new shapes: "It ended in Uttar Pradesh. / It had to. / You can't go around the world / attacking people with balloons / and expect to get away with it".

You can hear McGough's voice in these poems; not just his speaking voice, but his poetic voice, poking gentle fun at pretension and shining his poemy torch in dark corners. At times the corners are very dark indeed, as in the Carol Ann Duffyish 'End of Story', where a squaddie remembers: "Night on the town. Blood on the streets. / Razor blades stitched into the lapels / of his crushed velvet jacket. // Headcase but funny with it. Not like Fitzy. / Now we're talking nasty bastards. / Four brothers and half a brain between them". At times the corners aren't all that dark, but still resonate, like the last stanza of the otherwise chirpy 'New Brooms': "Dust is the carpet of the contented, / The motto of ancient brooms / and of the folk who sit contentedly / waiting, in darkening rooms".

None of us want to admit it, but, as I mentioned earlier, McGough is getting on a bit now, and his poems reflect that greater maturity, reflecting on a life lived in the spotlight, a life lived in poetry, a life lived in the service of verse. There are poems in this book that will stand the test of time (an awful, awful test soon to be introduced to all schools, colleges, hospitals and old folks homes, which is a McGoughish idea if ever I had one) like the three 'Bad Day at the Ark' poems, where Noah and his family, in a heart-on-sleeve plea from McGough for the animal kingdom, regret the loss of creatures like the bambanolas and the quinquasauropods and (maybe it's a good thing) the killer butterflies.

As I said at the start, I'm a McGough fan, and I have to say that if it hadn't been for him and a few others like him, standing up in pubs and schools and universities all those years ago, then we would never have had the poetry boom we've got now, and poetry would be an intensely studied minority interest in a quiet backwater. There would be no NewGen, no New Rock and Roll, no New Audiences, no National Poetry Day, so next time you see The Big McG, thank him from all of us.

You can order this book POST-FREE from the PBS at £9.99. See p.94 for details.

TWO POEMS BY BRIAN JONES
SEVERAL FLAUBERTS

To commemorate his savage
unanaesthetised dissection of us
we have severally erected
(a phrase he would have stored
with the slippers and the frillies)
his body (bloated with distaste)
and noble head (screamingly pressured
by our predictabilities);
first, against a quay
where boats slither fish
(as if the world
were endlessly spewing);
then under a lamp
where moths collect
around assignations;
thirdly, in view
of a downtown cafe
and its surrounds of shadow.
As if hammered by hopelessness,
bits of these hims
(who feared fathering a child)
begin to flake and fall
as he endures an eternal
re-enactment of his spawn –
a parked car shuddering its springs,
a man brushing a kiss away
as if moths bothered his lips,
and somewhere out of sight
(but obsessively seen)
a black trickle from a beautiful dead mouth.

MONUMENT DES MAQUISARDS

Most things were witnesses:
these clay canisters
from which scraggy shoots extrude
like shoved-in unwatered bunches
would have been young then,
hornbeams springing towards their prime,

and that haughty house, three-storeyed,
that I prise from wild hedgerow,
has flaking shutters that must have been
opened or slammed
upon the event;
while these sixty-foot cherries,
fresh, perhaps, from a first fruiting,
received the jolt
of a dozen rifles.
This granite block came later,
where three names and their code-names
glitter like fool's gold.
A fourth, equally shot,
is Un Inconnu,
which word touches me
like the tap on the shoulder
I hope never to receive.

THREE POEMS BY ALISON BRACKENBURY
TURING'S BICYCLE

Dear Alan Turing, my knowledge is slight.
I read somewhere: when your bicycle chain
Shook loose, you would not fix it tight

You pedalled, you counted. At forty-one
Before the chain links rattled free
You sprang to the dust. You hooked them on.

You cracked war's codes, the mind's machine.
But you died young, by your own hand.
The chain unspooled in its oily sheen.

Such scanty signs. What to infer?
That we, less thoughtful than you were
Must hammer chains; re-code despair.

CUSTOMER

You do not know why I cried last night
Why the last sandwich sailed into the hedge.
You did not see the cat with smudged grey ruff
Freeze by my tyres, spring lightly to the edge.

You do not know my parents' Christian names,
My daughter's voice, or where I went to school
Nor tell from my too careful ironed out tone
Who I once loved; and who I think a fool.

I come in twice a week to pick through bread,
Choose cabbages, complain about the flu
Beg a stout box and melt into the rain
And so you think you know me. And you do.

EPIGRAMS

My Latin has left me,
which may be as well.
They were brute engineers
and their afterlife, hell.

Only one tag stays:
a bird with no wings.
"*In medias res*"
in the middle of things.

I am weighed down by parents,
made mad by my child.
The late sky is sleeting
the garden is wild.

I slump on a chair
in the last glow day brings.
In medias res
in the muddle of things.

BOB ROGERS
CLICHÉS

They are like Shaker furniture, or cool
clean sheets, or apples in a bowl;
and we need them still as we need
water, sunlight, loaves of bread, fresh air.
For we are all the same, as they say, under the skin,
and there is nothing new under the sun.
Rain still makes us wet. Pain still hurts.
We still live under the same sun, moon
and stars. The same birds still sing,
from the same clouded or unclouded skies.
Leaves still come promptly with the spring
and fall at fall. In spite of Heraclitus,
we still step into the same rivers, walk
the same shores, watch the same waves breaking
and the same five-toed footprints
disappearing in the sand.
We are still rattling the bars of the same
metaphysical cage, knowing for certain
only that we pass this way but once,
have just this single chance
to gather rosebuds, to eat, drink and be merry . . .

At the world's end, or the end of the world,
there are no glittering prizes, no gold stars,
no apples, oranges or lollipops
awarded by the bored and blasé gods;
In the "eternal silence of those
infinite spaces", we shall fade like smoke
and all that we have ever said
will sound like rhubarbrhubarbrhubarbrhu . . .

BOB KAVEN
LOUIE LOUIE

My vowels roll like Northeastern Ohio, and you might
Slice your fingers on my consonants.
I can smell my own nerves burn.
At night, hazardous shapes hang above the Dempsey

Dumpsters in the alleyways of Somerville, Massachusetts,
Aimlessly whistling a tune
Deaf imitation
Of a Bach tocatta. The notes smudge their fingerprints

All over my face and smell metallic as a buzzing
Chain link fence on a cold night around
An electrical installation. Yes,
They smell like cut aluminum, these knots of flavor

Redistributing themselves like wealth all over my tongue.
My tongue is stained with memory
Like blueberries.
And Ann Schumacher of Canton, Ohio: She went on

To marry my cousin, Andy Lavin, of Canton, Ohio,
Though I can hardly remember the pageboy cut
She wore all through fifth grade.
It's simply gone. Actually, I remember too much

Too clearly, but when I think, all the objects of thought
Accordion like a car wreck . . .
My agoraphobia started
In the middle of my sixth grade dance, when the Deejay

Laid his needle in the groove and the speakers growled
Louie Louie. Caveat Emptor: We all wrote
Our own texts. Everyone's groin
Developed a subcutaneous flutter as the mathematical

Rituals of understanding agitated the airwaves
Above our brows, and the future
Became apparent. The rented
Deejay's simple gesture laid me out, unconscious

As an overmatched boxer. There I stood, outside my body,
Addressing myself. *Hoo baby!* I said,
This may go on forever, while
Everywhere around me a small industrial town in Ohio

Levitated with its cargo of memory. There I stood,
Like a stevedore, half gone in exhaustion
And wiping sweat thick as Vaseline
From my forehead, while the entire town became musical,

Freighting its load of numbers lightly as a Bach tocatta
Into a sky illuminated by torches three shifts a day.
Louie Louie, it sang,
And then whatever might have been the words that followed.

PATTY SCHOLTEN
DAY-TRIPPERS

translated from the Dutch by James Brockway

The truly adapted members of the nation,
the day-tripper tribe who do as others do,
are out to test my powers of toleration:
today the trip includes, of course, the zoo.

In training-gear like violent neon-lighting,
(no animal here could equal such display)
with kids for ever bawling, screaming, fighting,
in t-shirts shouting "Shit!" "Drop dead!" "No Way!"

The creatures they have come to stare at here
are imprisoned at our doing – ours the blame,
Evolution's two-legged heroes that we are.

To get away from here is all my aim.
I search in vain to get a breath of air,
I look around me, hang my head in shame.

PETER ARMSTRONG
STEEL GUITAR GEOGRAPHY

Since it's proven: *We're All Lonely*,
all confessees at that same roadside bar,
all biblically athirst
in the dry places of the heart;

make mine a bitter;
lead me from the jukebox weeping;
wed me to the Queen of Nowhere
whose sorrow is for keeps

II
And here's Safety, Nebraska, population us,
its houses wagon-ringed against the night,
a wheatscape dark enough
to show these window-lights from space.

Or should the moon ignite
the gravel at the side of the road,
surely this is where we longed to be:
not less lonely, but perfected in it.

III
After line dancing at the Masonic
cats' eyes half the darkness;
the telephone wires' deep harmonic
plays it how it is

ALAN BROWNJOHN
DUTY POEM

Avoiding the cluttered table, I pause awkwardly.
It isn't the gift of the image of August snow
Threading through the foreground steam that rises now
From the drink held to my lips. And it's not,
This time, from just a pleasure in pausing. But
Because I have seen one truth concerning Duty

– It need not be an escarpment one has decided
To draw deliberate breaths for, about to see
If muscles and sinews have the energy.
And it isn't so much the case of having to set
Aside some advantage one plotted for months to get.
It's the tiny inertias that ought to be roused and tidied

– And when that's done – Mankind! Such a flat
Smooth, emptied table-top is within one's range . . .
Was ever anything so clean, clear, strange
-ly resolute? Stretching for miles in front of the eyes
Without reproach, or guilt, or compromise?
. . . And you wish, you wish, you wish it would stay like that.

SMITA AGARWAL
AT FORTY

At forty she finds out how redundant emotion
is in the living of life. At nine –
the passing away of a puppy: sobbing the only option.
At sixteen, heartbreak: her boyfriend whines
he's leaving town. At twenty one she tells herself now she's too
grown-up; learns to transpose distress to a pinching shoe.

At thirty three her marriage is nosediving;
the extended family is weighing
down heavily upon her. Her children are
fractious. Colleagues are vicious. Her car
breaks down very often. The WC is
clogged. At thirty eight she loses her dad to diabetes.

Crying gets her nowhere. Tears have lost their zing.
Malleable-mop-up-mom has become a rational thing.

REVIEWS

Yow-trummle, scoogie, bawaw and derf

DAVID WHEATLEY ON KATHLEEN JAMIE

KATHLEEN JAMIE

Jizzen

Picador, £6.99
ISBN 1 9000 7240 8

CAN INCOMPREHENSION PLAY a part in poetic enjoyment? Words like "glar", "thole" or "clabber" litter the work of Seamus Heaney, conveying an agreeable frisson of Irishness to readers who don't understand them, but never to the point of making a poem entirely opaque. Even the notorious 'Broagh' is more arch than intimidating about how foreigners can't pronounce that tricky "gh" sound. Now compare MacDiarmid's 'Water Music': "Lively, louch, atweesh, atween, / Auchimuty or aspate, / Threidin' through the averins / Or bightsom in the aftergait...". It doesn't have quite the same effect: here the opacity is the whole point. My Penguin *Selected MacDiarmid* wouldn't have meant much to me as a student without a glossary for words like yow-trummle ("cold weather after sheep-shearing"), scoogie, bawaw and derf. MacDiarmid drifted increasingly to English in his later work, but never went as far as Robert Crawford or W. N. Herbert, who do their own annotating and even append English translations to poems in Scots. The problems with this are of a different order from authors like Sorley MacLean self-translating from Gaelic: what is the point of "search(ing) dictionaries for gorgeous defunct fragments (...) mak(ing) things up", as Herbert says he does, if not to get away from standard English, not instantly translate back into it?

One poet who has avoided the compulsion to theorize on her use of language in this way is Kathleen Jamie. If she feels torn between Scots and English, she has always dealt with it remarkably well: poems like 'Lucky Bag' and 'Bairnsang' from her excellent new collection *Jizzen* are at a lived-in extreme in their use of Scots from the post-MacDiarmid "lexomania" Don Paterson has spoken of. Jamie is a poet marvellously and unselfconsciously at home with her idiom. An unpostmodern preference for directness over obliquity has characterised her work in other areas too, her political poems for instance. Jamie's devolution poem is 'On the Design Chosen for the New Scottish Parliament Building by Architect Enric Miralles', which manages the trick of having a title almost three times longer than the poem: "An upturned boat / – a watershed."

If Jamie is direct though, it's not because she simplifies her often ambitious subjects. In 'Forget It' she tackles the resistance of her mother to her childhood curiosity about the past: the young Jamie's boast that in school "We done the slums today!" is answered with "Some history's better forgot". Some awkward questions to her mother about her family ("Why happened about my granddad? Why / did Agnes go? How / come you don't know") go unanswered, but instead of using them for an intergenerational stand-off *à la* Tony Harrison, Jamie ends the poem with a poignant image of the modest luxuries by which the family's escape from the bad old times is measured, her mother working part-time in Debenham's "to save for Christmas, / the odd wee / luxury, our first / foreign / holiday". It's just one example of how Jamie is able to make a point about politics and class without hammy indignation or sloganeering.

Jamie has spoken in interview of feeling "so constrained with the palaver of labelling I just bugger off abroad where nobody knows and nobody cares", but the travel poems in *Jizzen* don't escape from Scotland and questions of Scottish identity, just as it took the Queen of Sheba to sort Scotland out in her last book. 'Hackit', 'The Graduates' and 'The Pioneers' tackle emigration with the sort of clear-eyed perceptiveness we've come to expect from Jamie: a museum photograph of a Canadian emigrant cabin conjures a scene of "the axe and plough, the grindstone, / the wife by the cabin door / dead, and another sent for". In 'The Black and White Minstrel Show' she learns a lesson about gender and foreignness while singing in a school concert: why is it only the boys who get to be black, she wonders, looking into "the astonishing whites of their eyes"?

But the real centre of *Jizzen* (which means childbed, as I needed to be told) is a group of poems about motherhood. After seeing off 'The Bogey-wife', "who can smell babies", Jamie gives us a series of remarkably unself-centred lyrics in 'Ultrasound': her wish for her son, her "wee toshie man", in 'Prayer', is that "this new heart must outlive my own". In her poem 'Ceist na Teangan'/ 'The Language Issue' Nuala Ní Dhomhnaill compared her poem to a Moses basket left to drift downstream, into the lap (in Paul Muldoon's translation) "of some Pharoah's daughter". In Jamie's splendid 'The Tay Moses' it is her son who takes to the water, with the poet in hectic pursuit:

> slamming
> the car's gears,
> spitting gravel on tracks
> down between berry-fields,
> engine still racing, the door wide
> as I run toward her, crying
> LEAVE HIM! Please,
> it's okay, he's mine.

Jamie returns to political themes before the end of the book with her "watershed" poem and the amusing 'Interregnum', all of which goes to suggest how easily public and private mingle in her work. The passion to communicate we find in these poems is epitomized by the passion she brings to the act of feeding a child in the short lyric 'Bolus'. Like the rest of *Jizzen*, it makes for nourishing fare:

> So little of the world is bequeathed
> through us, our gifts,
> instead, are passed among the living
> – like words, or the bolus
> of chewed bread
> a woman presses with her tongue
> into the gorgeous open mouth of her infant.

You can order this book POST-FREE from the PBS at £6.99. See p.94 for details.

Reboring the Canon

by William Scammell

The Oxford Book of English Verse
Edited by Christopher Ricks
OUP, £20
ISBN 0 1921 4182 1

AUDEN, QUOTED ON the back cover, once said that Christopher Ricks is "exactly the kind of critic every poet dreams of finding". Dead ones more than live ones, perhaps. He's one of the best close readers we have, like his hero Empson, but it comes at the price of mannerism and a good many etiolated puns. See, for example, his eighty-page essay on Geoffrey Hill's use of hyphens (collected in *The Force of Poetry*), scrupulous to the point of insanity. See also the scholarship brought to bear on Eliot's juvenilia in the bulky apparatus to *Inventions of the March Hare*, or the promising but slightly evasive readings of the major poems in *T.S. Eliot and Prejudice*. Likewise when he gets Beckett or Bob Dylan between his teeth he doesn't let go very easily. This is fine up to a point – the point, usually, where the anatomist turns shaman and goes off into a cognitive devil dance all his own. Then a sort of proxy creativity sets in, which never quite convinces. He's fond of quoting Johnson on the critic's duty to "improve opinion into knowledge", which Eliot modulates (with Leavis's approval) into that phrase about "the common pursuit of true judgement".

Admirable stuff to fling at the relativists who curl up on Tracey Emin's bed with the latest slim monodrama set in a Yorkshire bus station. So too is Ricks's declaration that "poets have proved to be the best critics", and his endorsement of such as "Jonson... Dryden, Johnson, Coleridge, Arnold, and Eliot" as the best of the poet-critics, though Wordsworth is a notable absentee from the list, and so are Sidney, Campion, Milton, Keats, Shelley, Hopkins and Yeats, not to mention such recent practitioners as Empson and Jarrell,

Following in the footsteps of (Sir) Arthur Quiller-Couch (1900) and (Dame) Helen Gardner (1972), Ricks presents and modifies the canon according to his lights, while acknowledging that his role as compere makes him feel, "in the rueful Americanism, kinda humble and kinda proud". What's new is the inclusion of dramatic poetry from the golden age – chunks of Marlowe, Shakespeare, Webster and Tourneur – together with nursery rhymes, prose poems, hymns, nonsense verse, limericks and clerihews, and, on half a dozen occasions, original and revised versions of the same poem (e.g. Yeats's 'The Sorrow of Love'). This last is a fine indulgence for specialists but the space would surely have been better spent on more poets and/or poems. The same goes, as far as I'm concerned, for limericks and Bentley's clerihews.

A few late-medieval lyrics get the book under way, plus Gower, Langland, Lydgate, and not very much Chaucer. Just over four pages, in fact, less than any other major figure in the book, and some minor ones. This set me off on the numbers game, and here, for what it's worth, is Ricks's league table: Chaucer 4, Spenser 10, Marlowe 5, Shakespeare 19, Donne 7, Jonson 6, Herbert 5, Milton 12, Marvell 8, Dryden 7, Rochester 5, Swift 7, Pope 8, Johnson 6, Blake 10, Burns 7, Wordsworth 13, Coleridge 16 (two poems only, the Mariner complete and 'Kubla Khan'), Byron 4, Shelley 6, Clare 2, Keats 9, Tennyson 3, Browning 5, Arnold 4, Clough 2, Christina Rossetti 15, Swinburne 7, Hardy 7, Hopkins 9, Housman 4, Yeats 5, Kipling 4, Edward Thomas 4, Owen 3, Rosenberg 2, Graves 4, Austin Clarke 5 (partly as translator), Bunting 1, Empson 4, Auden 4, MacNeice 2, Dylan Thomas 3, Larkin 5, Hughes 3, Hill 3, Heaney 5 (much of it wasted on 'Ugolino', his Dante translation).

There are various foolishnesses here, such as the overestimate of Swift, Johnson, Rossetti (the whole of 'Goblin Market') Empson, the under-estimate of MacDiarmid (nothing from *The Drunk Man*), Bunting (nothing from 'Briggflatts'), Auden, MacNeice, Hughes. The twentieth-century selection, in fact, is a mess, and the closer it approaches the present the worse it gets. If Heaney why not Mahon, Longley, Harrison, Dunn? Where are Robert Garioch, Sorley Maclean, Mackay Brown, Norman MacCaig? Where's Causley? Why waste two whole pages on Thwaite's 'We are too many' poem? – fine as a magazine squib but plain silly in this rigorously selective temple of the muses. Good to find Norman Cameron, but not one of his best. No Bernard Spencer, or Alan Ross. No Roy Fisher. None of Auden's deadly light verse, too much of Betjeman's and Stevie Smith's. (The Preface talks of "the hauntings of Blake and Stevie Smith", as though there were some subtle link between the visionary and the whimsical. No 'Soldiers Bathing' by F.T. Prince, only the stiffly academic 'An Epistle to a Patron'. Only one short poem from Alun Lewis (not at his best), two from Keith Douglas, nothing at all from Roy Fuller. No Thomas Blackburn or W. S. Graham, no Redgrove or D.M. Black, no Patricia Beer, Anne Stevenson, Fleur Adcock. No Plath either. The Larkin selection is poor – no 'Arundel Tomb', no 'Whitsun Weddings', no 'Less Deceived', no 'Toads', visited or revisited, no 'Talking in Bed', no 'Next, Please' or 'Church Going'.

Betjeman and Empson get handles stuck on to them on the Contents page: Sir John, Sir William, etc. In which case why not "Ted Hughes OM" and "Joe Bloggs OBE"? Grigson pointed out long ago that this sort of pomp is utterly out of place in poetry, which is its own reward, if anything ever was. You can imagine Lords Milton and Wordsworth, Sir Robert Burns, and Baron Clare spinning in their graves.

Which takes us safely back to the past, and firmer ground. I was pleased to discover William Alabaster (1568-1640) and his two petrarchan sonnets, though there's no room for Edward Benlowes or Thomas Browne, no elegy on Donne from Carew (we get the epitaph on Lady Mary Villiers instead, and the famous 'Song'), no Margaret Cavendish. A good selection from Donne, and from the other well-known Metaphysicals. Richard Corbett's ballad on 'The Faeryes Farewell', on the other hand, is an anti-commonwealth squib that belongs only in the history books. As for the six poems by Matthew Prior, I'd far rather have the jolly verse of

Charles Cotton, who is represented by 'Evening Quatrains', a poem as dull as its title. William Roscoe's 'The Butterfly's Ball and the Grasshopper's Feast' is on the twee side too, and metrically inert.

The wondrous Alexander Pope gets chopped up into bits: bits from the *Essay on Criticism*, *The Rape of The Lock*, three of the Epistles, and the *Dunciad*, plus an epitaph and an epigram. Better to have printed the whole of the 'Epistle to Arbuthnot', and let Bathurst and Burlington go hang. Dryden's chopped liver too, as he must be when anthologised. Mary Leapor, who died at 24 (1722-1746), is in with 'Mira's Will', which made me look up her three poems in Roger Lonsdale's *Oxford Book of Eighteenth Century Verse*. Jean Elliot's (1727-1805) 'The Flowers of the Forest' was new to me too, and she's not in Lonsdale.

Blake gets a good showing, mostly from the *Songs of Innocence and Experience*. There's a song too from 'An Island in the Moon', but no *Marriage of Heaven and Hell*, that wonderful nest of paradoxes for old Nobodaddy to lay his eggs in. Passages from the long visionary poems (which had a bad effect on Ginsberg, and indeed didn't do Blake himself much good) tend to be the sexy bits ("Why a tender curb upon the youthful burning boy! / Why a little curtain of flesh on the bed of our desire?" – from *Thel*).

Thence to the Romantics and Victorians. I've never got round properly to Winthrop Mackworth Praed (1802–1839) or James Clarence Mangan (1803–1849), though I know their names. This taster made me want to read more, and suggested that Clough's distinctive voice in *Amours de Voyage*, and in his light verse, isn't quite so isolated or without precedent as I'd thought. Clough himself gets only three short poems, and Matthew Arnold not much more. Three sonnets from Meredith's 'Modern Love' sequence remind you how irritating poets can be who are good but not quite good enough. (Meredith's wife, high-spirited daughter of Thomas Love Peacock, got involved, and eventually ran away with Another Man, the chap who painted that famous picture of Chatterton on his deathbed. Her life was actually more interesting than Meredith's poem-cycle. See Diane Johnson's *Lesser Lives* for an excellent account of the whole imbroglio.) Meredith's 'Lucifer in Starlight' is also included, probably because Eliot makes use of its last line: 'The army of unalterable law'.

No 'Neutral Tones' from Hardy, that wonderful bitter love poem, and no 'I Look Into My Glass' to round him off. Instead we get several anthology chestnuts ('The Darkling Thrush', 'Afterwards', etc) and four of the best of the posthumous love poems to Emma, or rather about Emma and to himself.

Robert Louis Stevenson, I notice, uses the word "gyre" in an untitled poem, or extract (no. 594). Did Yeats know about this? No dates are given, and there are no notes, so we are left to wonder. Patrick Kavanagh is missing, Ricks tells us, because his executors are still squabbling about the rights. His inclusion of 'Interrogativa Cantilena' (1641), on the other hand, tells us that English nonsense verse was alive and well long before its heyday in the nineteenth century. Only eight lines from *The Waste Land* are allowed in ('Death by Water'), only the skating episode from *The Prelude*, and only the closing choral sonnet from *Samson Agonistes*. Wouldn't the vast riches of English poetry be worth two volumes rather than one?

Though it's well printed and bound, and got up handsomely in a parchment jacket, I can't help thinking that this prestigious book would have been given a larger format, more generous margins, and a greater number of pages if it had been produced in America. See the recent doorstopper *World Poetry* from Norton; or compare their modern slim volumes with ours. Still there's an enormous amount here to enjoy, as well as to scratch your head over. Look up W. E. Henley's 'To WR', the one that begins "Madam Life's a piece in bloom / Death goes dogging everywhere. / She's the tenant of the room, / He's the ruffian on the stair". Better than Fenton and Cope, or worse? Are the trochees a trifle glib? What do you make of the extended metaphor (as the poem goes on) of life as a hooker? Is Housman as good as Ricks thinks he is, or stuck in post-adolescent pangs of tremendous pastiche? Will the jury ever file back in and agree on Kipling? Were Larkin and Hughes major or minor as compared with the 1680s, 1780s, 1880s? Is the pluralism we all preen ourselves on, technical and cultural, any improvement on 17th century pithiness or Augustan propriety, flexing its pecs in immaculate pentameters? Do we write as much waffle about human rights, or about science, as the Victorians did about God? Is the long poem gone forever? Discuss.

You can order this book POST-FREE from the PBS at £20. See p.94 for details.

REVIEWS

Death-Struck

by Iain Bamforth

THOMAS LOVELL BEDDOES
Selected Poems
Carcanet, £8.95
ISBN 1 857 54408 0

GOTHIC, MACABRE, DISDAINFUL, Thomas Lovell Beddoes is one of the oddest figures in English poetry. Ezra Pound called him "the prince of Morticians", Graham Greene the "filibustering medical poet". Dr Death might be our contemporary moniker. He died 150 years ago in a Basle hospital after a dose of curare. "I am food for *what I am good for* – worms," he wrote in his suicide note. Cult references to him crop up in odd places like Dorothy Sayer's murder-mystery 'Have His Carcase', though if he is known today it is for a single exquisite anthology piece, 'Dream-Pedlary'. John Ashbery is a fan. He was more than half in love with easeful death, "death-struck" before Freud posited such a thing; it is Beddoes, rather than the apothecary's assistant Keats, who has a more obvious claim to be remembered as the pre-eminent doctor-poet of the Romantic era.

Beddoes (1803-49) came from a distinguished free-thinking family. His aunt was the novelist Maria Edgeworth. His father, Dr John Lovell Beddoes, scientist and inventor, was a friend of Coleridge and colleague of Sir Humphry Davy; he discovered nitrous oxide. Together with James Watt and Josiah Wedgwood he founded the famous Bristol Pneumatic Institute. In his time Beddoes senior was notorious as a supporter of the French Revolution. He died when his son was 5, a man so unconventional in his intellectual habits he dissected animals in front of his children. Beddoes followed the family tradition in medicine, choosing in 1825 to study in Göttingen, a Hanoverian university with a strong medical faculty. His imagination seems to have flourished in the atmosphere of German idealism, its Jacobean strain becoming even more pronounced. It was at this time, studying with the famous anatomist Blumenbach, that he started work on his masterpiece *Death's Jest Book*, a surreal mortality play. It is an oddly jaunty work,

a laugh in the face of death spurred in part by his signal failure, as he wrote to his friend Kensall, to find "any kind of shadow of a proof or probability of an after-existence, both in the material and immaterial nature of man". His loss of conventional Enlightenment faith, and inability to find an intellectual solution for it, resembles that of another young anatomist-writer, Georg Buchner, best known for his play *Woyzeck*. Buchner's father, a doctor too, also used perform dissections with his son as assistant. Both anatomist-writers may well have met in the 1830s – an interesting coincidence of minds, since they were both political radicals. What we would recognise today as democrats.

Death's Jest Book did not go down well when he showed it to friends in England. Like all his dramatic pieces it is unstageable, as if his characters were untethered forms of an idea. It is shot through with brilliant passages: Beddoes' Old Adam – the "carrion crow" – seems to anticipate Ted Hughes' baleful anthropomorphic creature of the same name. "What is the lobster's tune when he is boiled?" a central character asks, recalling Belacqua in one of Beckett's most famous stories. A memorably creepy sequence is entitled 'The Oviparous Tailor'. It is all very Jacobean – "cool as an ice-drop in a dead man's eye" as another play has it. *DJB* proved to be Beddoes' albatross. Having set out to produce a revenge play in the Kidd or Webster mould, its writing was continually interrupted by sardonic, incongruous elements – as if the spell of its creation was "read backwards". Letters of the mid-1820s to his friend Kelsall, with their mention of "windeggs" and galvanism make him sound like Faust. Or perhaps Dr Frankenstein, that famous novel of forbidden knowledge written by another child of a freethinking family, the 19-year old Mary Shelley, wife of the poet Beddoes admired above all his contemporaries. The eye she cast on a generation of self-proclaimed (male) geniuses and domestic tyrants was, it must be said, more coldly seeing than Beddoes'.

Depressed at his literary failure, Beddoes got drunk in public and was expelled from university. He completed his MD at Wurzburg, though he was later deported by the Bavarian government in 1833 as a political agitator. He lived in Zurich for seven years, respected as a man of science and letters, but increasingly eccentric; when its liberal government fell he was forced to become an intellectual vagrant. His last visit to London was remembered years later for his drunken attempt to set fire to the Drury Lane playhouse with a lighted five-pound note in protest at what he saw as the shoddiness of British theatre. He ended up, on the invitation of a friend, in Basle: it was no doubt an apt choice, as the city from which Death danced out in the series of famous medieval woodcuts. A year after the 1848 wave of revolutions across Europe he finally succeeded in killing himself having previously botched an attempt to open his arteries and had a leg amputated as a consequence; it was – ironically – the year which saw the Swiss federation guarantee the kind of liberties he had fought for as a younger man.

Beddoes's reputation ought to be disinterred from the oblivion he thought was "not so bad once one's got into the knack of it". It would be fascinating if documents turn up some day proving that he did meet Buchner on his travels. More of a realist than Beddoes (though he remained unknown in Germany until the First World War), Buchner attributed the crisis of Reason in the wake of the French Revolution to Cartesianism – to its mystification of mind and reduction of body to something resembling an animate cadaver, a thralldom not entirely unfamiliar to modern medicine. Beddoes, on the other hand, seems to have set out to prove that death was a sham: *LJB*'s recklessness suggests that as a young medical student in Göttingen he must have gone through a dark night of the soul: his intellectual search to understand the how was actually a deeply emotional need to grasp the why.

More information can be obtained from the Thomas Lovell Beddoes Society
http://www.nortexinfo.net/McDaniel/tlb.htni

You can order this book POST-FREE from the PBS at £8.95. See p.94 for details.

Forces of Gravity

by Katherine Gallagher

TRACY RYAN

The Willing Eye
Bloodaxe, £6.99
ISBN 1 85224 506 9

THIS IS WEST Australian Tracy Ryan's first book to be published in the U.K. It is a powerful and assured collection, resonant with passionate, original and compelling explorations of the wonders and vulnerabilities of being. The poems are highly personal yet relentlessly reach out to the "other", delineating the borders of self – self in a landscape as human, lover, parent – always with an acute sense of the foreign. Her journey into other languages via translation is part of this. In the book's final sequence, she examines the notion of translation (debates whether *Traduire, c'est trahir* – wonderful pun!) as being like a marriage, a chess game – worth the risks, albeit concluding that "Only the capacity to love / otherness / can bring us there / finally". ('The Translation').

'Lunar Eclipse', based on a childhood experience of being unable to sleep due to the heat and thus staying outdoors ("even sheets too dense / for the body's escape"), captures some of Ryan's preoccupations – particularly, that of human fragility: "we lay upright on a planet / facing other planets hung in the vast / blackness – not horizontal under sky / but part of it. All footholds slippery, / grounding provisional, the earth was then / a vehicle over whose actual course / we'd no control, we had to travel blind". A heightened sense of discovery limns these poems as Ryan ties wide-ranging visual detail into juxtapositions and ironies in intelligent, deeply-felt, tightly-wrought free verse.

In an author's statement about her poetry in the recently-published Australian anthology, *Landbridge*, Ryan says, "Comments on possible directions are quickly dated: I find out as I go along". Her further comment, including a quote from Cixous: "Writing neither from England nor from Australia but returning 'from afar, from always: from *without*, from the heath where witches are kept alive...' (Cixous, *The Laugh of the Medusa*)" is probably the best pointer to where Ryan is at. For these are poems of place that link the quest for identity and a life lived to the full, even at the very edges of experience, with a piercing appreciation of the vulnerabilities therein.

This is especially evident in poems for her daughter where the child may be troubled, as in 'Splinter' – "this sliver" is too fine, and in too far, for finger or tweezer to call it back, so the mother, remembering the child in herself, must finally remove it:

Tomorrow, I'll buy a needle,

recall my own mother running
pin-tip through flame,
the silver clouded
to rainbowed black, . . .

Holding this memory up
like a map, I will enter
the merest surface
of her little hand to find
the random invader, . . .

later reassuring her daughter that "our bodies are solid but open / at every pore".

This balancing of precariousness and gentle protectiveness runs throughout the book, sustaining moods of intimacy and tenderness; it is again pointed to in 'Edge' where the hazards are suburban ice and snow. Ryan's eye for a celebratory image is remarkable – as in 'Stork Picture'. Her child has drawn a stork's nest and:

Tonight she'll dream
Of a roof with broad, warm wings
Folded in.

The conceits are a delight. "Glasses" (spectacles) are "clear eggshells" that might accidentally be walked on ('Portrait with Glasses'). A lovebite is a "Dark corsage I can't / unpin,. ." ('Bite'). In childbirth, the body opens, "...my edges raw but soft / like pages cut for the first time". ('Acts of Faith'). Vital and erotic. One is reminded of Cassian and Olds and the two Emilys – Bronte and Dickinson.

In Australia, Ryan (b. 1964) already has quite an established reputation as a poet. In 1987, she won the prestigious Mattara Poetry Prize. She has also published two collections, *Killing Delilah* (1994) and *Bluebeard in Drag* (1996), and a novel *Vamp* (1997).

Her earlier books concentrated much more on myths and masks to suggest a multiplicity of subjects and voices. In the poem, 'Killing Delilah' the mask is being stripped away:

I thought her face was my own face,
put faith in her social graces –
she was always in demand.
But sooner or later someone
was bound to ask for me.

The six parts of *The Willing Eye* interface around aspects of personal experience: Breath, Bite, Excursions, Near, Life Halved & Parted, and Partial Visions, giving an overall effect of a unified and focused approach. The eye is always there, guiding the poem's voice along a range of feeling from fearfulness and disquiet to love and the simplest joys in these moving, technically-deft poems. Tracy Ryan is aware that "the willing eye" can be fooled: "a hopeless romantic that / can only be cheated" ('Trompe l'oeil'). But she's ready to risk it.

You can order this book POST-FREE from the PBS at £6.95. See p.94 for details.

TRACY RYAN
CLINICAL

Indignity of death wanting
to enter this way
here, of all places, where they flowed
with essence of goodness

but where would you choose, exactly
to let him in?

Clamped, flattened & scanned
from every angle
resistant, like fuzzy barcodes or
bad blueprints

guided by pain alone, the bumps
that ache like milk
no longer needed
but are something different

skewered & sampled & then restored
to personhood
each woman leaves dejected
or elated, nothing between them.

An ink ring, indelible
where he made it a thing
so it wouldn't feel wrong to do this.

A little gauze cross, like a botched
suture, to mark the spot.

JOHN GALLAS
JOSEF

Most likely as a spook, he murmured down
one day when I was halfway up an Alp
and hovered in the snowy sunshine. "Help!"
I yelled. I slipped and fell. I saw him frown.
"Of all the brave delights that I was born
to pass to you spun in my genes", he growled,
"I'm sorry –" – tears filled up his eyes. I scowled
and scrabbed in the snow. "Ach dear, forlorn,
distracted Man, what slug hides in the rose
of enterprise!" I gasped. "An unsound heart".
He mooned away. My crampons fell apart.
Is this some kind of judgement then? God knows.
I reached the top and rested. *I* don't know.
The valleys, steeps and ridges shone with snow.

LOLA HASKINS
THE MAKER OF LINES

I

HOW I BECAME AN ENGINEER

When I was little, they gave me dot to dots
with black points scattered like stars in reverse.
But they made a mistake: they numbered the stars.
I saw the elephant they wanted me to see. I saw
the dog. I saw the igloo, the fur round the Eskimo's
floating smile. Why bother, I said.
                                But then one day
(I was five), I tucked my tongue between my teeth
and I blacked the numbers out. Then I pressed hard
between the dots, with lines so strong they veed
the page. My mother said the pictures looked like
nothing. Not to me. They looked like lines.
And I made them. And they could not be erased.

II

THE SEED ROAD

*In order to generate support for the first cross-country
highway, stretches of roads were improved in rural communities
to show the public how comfortable travel could be.*

We poured a batter of rock and sand.
We wet the slowly setting slabs, worked
them smooth with 2 X 4s, laid them
end to end like truth set down, over
the rutted tracks the locals called road.
And all at once their bones stopped
jittering. Their throats cleared.
They were like anyone who has lived
with pain. They did not understand
how hard they'd braced, until they felt
their shoulders loosen, as if something
were unfolding inside, yawning,
stretching sleepy wings.

III

THE ENGINEERS HEAR FROM THE PUBLIC

We divided the land in squares and looked
at the map through them, the way my wife
might look through her veil at church. And
we listened in a row of suits, as one by one
you approached the microphone. And
as you spoke, we drew: a sprawl of lines,
like fish net spread on hills and plains.
We gave you what you asked. You wanted
to be somewhere else, and soon. But let me
make this clear. We never said you were
anything but fish. We never promised things
would be different when you arrived.

IV

HIGHWAYS

Highways crack with weather and are not repaired.
Their bridges moan, as the slow damp gnaws
them red. Where are the young engineers,
their starched sleeves pushed to the elbows,
the curled black hairs on their forearms electric?
In the light of day
        the salesman in his battered
Nissan, trunk crammed with samples, his
shirts on a rod in the back seat, must cross
broken glass when he turns into the new city,
past the airport where each jet's roar comes
to nothing in the blue air.

ROBERT SAXTON
THE EEL-FARE

A transparent willow-leaf the sea tossed
    Around the Faroes in 1904: one of millions,
    The fortunate, many more millions lost.
I hatched a dream of tracing a thread
    Of ever-diminishing eel larvae
Out to some unexpected sea-bed
    Where eels whelp in their millions
In fathomless, fecund conspiracy.

When war curtails the study of zoology,
    As with eel studies, animals sometimes
    Enjoy a holiday, sometimes flee
From guns in terror of their lives,
    Or their habitat's blasted off the map.
Men die in pieces, far from their wives.
    In hunger one might sometimes
Grope for an alluringly waisted eel-trap

At night in a mill-leat beside a willow-root,
    Poaching like silent death if possible,
    Alert for the possible creak of a jackboot
Or a huddled sniper's ominous click.
    The fusillade of water-droplets sends
Elvers darting every which way in panic.
    Empty! Hunger conjures impossible
Doves from a dovecote where the stream wends

Past a farmhouse whose black bomb-wound
    Is nursed to nothing by the moonlit night.
The first night we honeymooned
    Doves like these attended, like bridesmaids
Bribed to stay after the wedding
    To loose their soft white cannonades
    Of wings upon the peaceful night,
Predictive nestlings of the tousled bedding.

Shelling has drained the stream in places
    Into underground diversions, but elvers
    Find on other elvers' bodies traces
Of moisture enough to make a ladder

Of dying comrades clinging to sheer
Lock walls up which the slithery armada
      Climbs, canal sides tiled with elvers,
Scaled with no less ease than waterfall or weir.

For the table, though, one favours the mature
      Eel, whose yellow has turned to silver,
      A glint of silver in the eye of the epicure
Imagining the moonless work at the Po's
      Mouth where the catch in a single night
Can be a thousand tons, in nets hung to foreclose
      The exodus of contraband silver
Smuggling out its gleam, unpacked by searchlight.

Far from the fighting sits the connoisseur.
      If he should happen to receive one day
      After a day a friend spends fishing, as douceur,
A gift of an eel in a bucket, let his thanks
      Include his countrymen at the front
In meadows smashed to sludge by rain and tanks
      Where reason fights to win, or live, the day,
And men like eels slither in warfare's effluent.

If he's to consummate this thoughtful tribute,
      First he must undress the thing,
      Something he's too decent not to fear – uproot
Its life from the ground of itself, in a dream
      Or fit of madness perform the kill
With a skewer in its head, hang it from a beam,
      Peel the glove of skin with pliers, then nothing
For it but the chopping into segments, jerking still.

In 1922 the thread of diminishing larvae
      Ended for me in the eastern part,
      The seaweedy part, of the Sargasso Sea –
The spawning ground, inched by the drift
      Of continents two thousand miles or more,
Straining the instincts of eels by a shift
      That pulls beginnings and endings apart,
Then back again by a miracle, like war.

SUSAN WICKS
DUCHESS OF MALFI

for Bridget

You are the one clear thing
in a world of purple
coils of bent wire and pillars,
eyes that glitter
under the lights. You enter
through a lace of gates,
touch your burning taper
to the candles, to a flame
that flickers out so fast –
you're taking a husband,
gorging on apricots –
now three growing children,
barely half an hour to separate
the first birth from the last.
You bid them farewell
as if you had lived already,
understood the ending –
three shadow-corpses swinging
on gauze, the rant and slaver
of madmen. *Let them come in.*
And then the loop of rope
on your own pale neck, the crack
as it tightens.
              So you are
put out, the gleaming dress
is laid to rest. Two hours
from unripe fruit
to old rope. Now we wait
for the flat dark
when you can stand and leave
unseen – the rope, the candlestick,
the chalice gathered up,
the wrought gates gaping open
on their silent hinges.

SELIMA HILL
LULU'S NIGHT OFF

Somebody's mouth is ejecting a spray of saliva
over the glittering kulfi-and-gin-coloured melon-balls
that tower above her toy-boys like a fountain
as my famous hostess guides me towards the kitchens
on the pretext of showing me Lulu's ingenious melon-scooper
and thence by a secret stair-case
to her room

where, closing the door
and suggesting I try on the ball-gown
she's smoothing out like an awkward shimmering lake
on a king-sized quilt of undulating satin,
she starts to unhook the hooks of my little bra –
but I'm deaf as a post to her pleas
and before she knows it

I'm sprinting away down the drive in a cloud of dust
home to my dog to be sick as a dog
like the tennis star
wasting away in a sheet
from Legionnaire's Disease
caught from a patron's decorative Water Curtain
everyone said at the time was *really sexy*.

VERNON SCANNELL
LEGAL TENDER

"Brown's made of money!" These words puzzled me
when I first heard them at the age of seven,
spoken by my grumpy Uncle Stephen.
Like a snowman's made of snow? How could he be?

Money, to me, was clinking metal, round –
ha'pennies and pennies that could buy you sweets;
the silver coins for more expensive treats
were rarely seen and almost never owned.

Each Christmas Day, before I grew too old,
I'd find, in stocking or on Christmas tree,
a small net scarlet bag and you could see
it held a dozen coins of glittering gold.

The gold, of course, was bogus, made of thin
shining foil, and yet its gleam was more
exciting than the aspect real cash wore:
it hinted sweet delight beneath the skin.

Perhaps my Uncle's Mr. Brown was made
of dollar bills, a faceless lightweight guy.
Once, I'm told, in Borneo they'd buy
goods with human skulls, a grisly trade.

Not sinister, but every bit as strange
were feather-money in New Hebrides,
salt in Ethiopia, oxen in Greece;
all, long ago, were media of exchange.

Today, approaching the Millennium's close,
the paper and the clinking stuff is less
often used for trading, though I'd guess
more is stashed away than you'd suppose,

stored in little glittering hoards beneath
old mattresses and under creaking floors,
concealed in socks inside camphoric drawers
among old photos, hairpins and false teeth.

Although ignored, forgotten and unspent
they keep some shine, survive their savers who,
whatever they were made of, had to bow
before Time's final disembellishment.

ROS BARBER
INSIDE OUT

Nightly she inserts
her diaphragm,
the gasp of the vowel
that ends her name,

full of hope and rubber.
Sundays the air
is crumbed
with sage and onion,

the wetted slap
of his muscular hands
stuffing the bird.
As he salts the skin

she perches between
place settings, thighs
parted like a mouth,
provoking her husband's

shudder; her gusset:
a baby's skull
tearing its bulk
out of the cavity.

How long has it been?
Meat should be tender,
surrender itself
from the bone.

He glazes with sweat,
anxiously presses
the breast to check
for the absence of blood.

DENNIS O'DRISCOLL
13

No one will sleep with 13.
His hotel suite is invariably single.
Allocated his airplane seat,
passengers make excuses, demand a move.
No one wants to live

under the same roof as 13:
they add 'A' as a safety barrier
or deny him entirely – a figure
airbrushed from history; elevators
rush straight from floor 12 to 14.

Fridays prove his undoing:
highway pile-ups earn him
a bad name;
            break-ups, mistakes,
lost contracts and umbrellas
are all laid at his barricaded door.

He craves a normal life, would
gladly settle down with long-legged 11
or curvaceous 9, would be faithful
even to the plainest 7, would
change his name by deed poll,

start all over elsewhere in the guise
of 31, if only he were not so greatly
needed as a scapegoat, if only his
detractors – once 13 themselves –
would concede their own share of the blame.

GAEL TURNBULL
TIME IS

Time is a fisherman and in his net we're not the ones
    that get away
and time's the landlord, when he calls we must obey
and tallyman, not much is on the house, mostly you've
    got to pay
and referee, so mark your man, shoot when you can,
    there'll be no action replay
and irrelevant, whatever time the clock says, it's
    always now this moment that's today.
So help yourself! There's no room service. You'll not
    get it handed to you on a tray.
The best is to arrive, enjoy the scene, last out the
    night but not to want to stay,
for time's the wall at which the blindfold prisoner
    stands to wait for break of day.
Hang on to that, time's measure, for if you can't
    you'd better get down on your knees and pray,
for time's the croupier. He turns the wheel. We place
    our bets. And sometimes win. Who knows? You may.
    I may.
Though straight or gay, no one makes time. For all
    that he looks an easy lay,
and bent or straight, all get it. Because time rules,
    O.K. or not O.K.
and when the party's done, it's time that calls the
    cab, hands us our coat, opens the door, and
    leads the way
whatever any one of us may say,
whatever song the band may chose to play,
however hard we join in on that chorus of
Delay, Delay, Delay.

Time of No Reply

by Sarah Wardle

NICK DRAKE

The Man in the White Suit
Bloodaxe, £6.95
ISBN 1 85224 488 7

THE MAN IN the White Suit won the Forward Prize for Best First Collection. It is easy to see why. Nick Drake shows a talent for capturing the suffering and loneliness of people, and the instantaneousness of events. Exiles and AIDS victims populate a book which moves from Eastern Europe after the collapse of Communism ten years ago to contemporary London. His Czech roots and friendships with AIDS victims add particularity and worldliness to his elegies and love poems. His sympathy even extends to Ceausescu's daughter, in whose room he sleeps: "I could almost / pity her, / spoiled ghost".

Drake's insights are plentiful, but he fits his imagery into concise language. In the opening poem, excitement during the 1968 Prague Spring of liberalisation is captured in the closing picture of revellers skinnydipping, "unpolitical and free". In 'Last Train' "a Circle Line refugee" is busking with foreign change at her feet: "an ear of wheat, a leaping fish, the wrong Queen". Drake has a sharp eye for metaphor and detail. In the title poem the Hotel Europa contains: "currency girls whose shrugged-off furs / hung savage from their chairs". In a skilful cultural cut-and-paste, he pictures Salome alongside Liberace. The reference to the Ealing Studios film might go over the heads of a younger generation, but the final image of loss is clear, when he is left alone with the apparently indestructible "white suit melting on me where I stood".

Film also surfaces in the collection's closing poem, in which he slips convincingly into the speech of a sound technician. Drake's knack for characterisation shows here, as in the portraits of historical characters, and sketches of dying and displaced persons. Two Czechoslovakian refugees — the poet, Ivan Blatny, and his own grandmother — are tenderly handled in a variety forms. In 'Cigarettes for Mr Blatny' Drake uses conversational, free verse to depict how he bribed the institutionalised Blatny to talk, whereas the rhymed ending to 'The Ghost Train' musically laments the distressed poet. In 'Six Studies of Anna Vondracek' rhyme plays a backing track to memorable photographic images, whilst the 'The Angel of History' is a free verse documentary of his grandmother's last days. Towards the end he sparingly records finding evidence in her diary of his own birth: "Boy born. Shopping. Tea".

The depth of feeling in his elegies for friends dying of Aids is reminiscent of Thom Gunn's *The Man with Night Sweats*, though Drake's descriptions are perhaps more subtle. 'The Very Rich Hours' employs an effective analogy with medieval books of hours to juxtapose "the very rich hours of the land of the living" with the subject's dying, but also to compare medieval chivalrous love with modern homosexual love. The warmth of a poem like 'The Cure' transcends sexuality. Audenesque in its formality, it is reminiscent of 'Stop all the clocks...':

Not a prayer for the dying, for you, for us, not
    crying, not yet.

Tonight only the clock, each concentrated second
    one tiny grain
in a thousand thousand parts
of rain.

In 'Ausonius and Paulinus' he tackles the timelessness of male friendship. Tutor and pupil have a bond reminiscent of Socrates and Plato, or Narziss and Goldmund. Through the voice of Paulinus, Drake creates an opening for some classic lines on love, but he cleverly subverts traditional expectations, as the addressee is neither a woman, nor God. He also plays with devotion in 'The Juke Box'. Here his coin is a votive offering, and the music, echoed in the poem's rhymes, is "the Harmony of the Spheres' 'All You Need Is Love'". It is an indication of his light touch that allusions to the Beatles, the moon landings and Ealing Studios can sit so comfortably alongside references to Archimedes, the Romans and Dr Johnson.

A quote from Samuel Johnson provides the epigraph for the collection: "An odd thought strikes me: / we shall receive no letters in the grave". This illuminates how we can read his book: as letters addressed to dead family and friends. Drake brings his characters to life. I shall look out for his strong voice in the next decade.

You can order this book POST-FREE from the PBS at £6.95. See p.94 for details.

The Way Things Are

by Paul Groves

The Forward Book of Poetry
Forward Publishing &
Faber and Faber, £7.95
ISBN 0 571 20220 9

BEYOND ANDY LOVELL'S nothingy cover design resides an anthology which will satisfy if not delight. Simon Armitage, Helen Dunmore, Penelope Shuttle, Erica Wagner (*The Times*), and John Walsh (*The Independent*) have done a fine job assembling some of the best practitioners of modern verse. William Sieghart's Preface and Armitage's Foreword set the tone: the former says, "we hope to help... confirmed sceptics understand how approachable and accessible... poetry can be". The latter highlights "eclecticism and pluralism", adding that the book portrays "A parade, rather than a race for the line". Armed with these articles of faith, one expects the contents to be largely understandable and one is not disappointed. There is little that is doctrinaire or wilfully difficult; plain diction and the Britain of comprehensive education and anti-elitism hold sway.

Jane Draycott, a contender for the Best Collection Prize with *Prince Rupert's Drop*, has entries notable for their emotional control; 'Dream' – from 'Braving the Dark' – succeeds where oneiric efforts generally fail through sloppiness or excess. Kate Clanchy's poems make sense, a prerequisite for any writing – surely – yet frequently overlooked or ignored. Carol Ann Duffy's work here is mesmerising, wacky, and egocentric ('The Devil's Wife' has sixty-nine references to self in sixty-six lines, whereas Jo Shapcott – also shortlisted – has none among the eighteen lines of 'Mandrake Pie').

In the Best First Collection category Matthew Caley's longish lacustrine effort is quietly spectacular and, like all this volume's successes, not lacking in ambition; Nick Drake scores with 'In Memory of Vincent Cox'; Christopher North provides the beautifully-precise 'The Dog' and the well-modulated, if strange, 'Hard Times'; and Christiania Whitehead's 'Angels' is particularly intelligent, reminding one how severe the competition can be these days.

In the Best Individual Poems section looms Caroline Carver's 'Horse Under Water', last year's National Poetry Competition winner. Although a remarkable piece of work, it leaves this reader uneasy, as if its creator – apparently a middle-class middle-aged white woman – were playing the ethnic-minority card it is politically correct these days to brandish. Nothing wrong with the ethnic minorities doing it, but for the rest of us to try is like appropriating their clothes. There is a fair bit of numerical itemisation – from 'Zero' (Robert Crawford's comical nineties take on the world of Peter Porter's 'sixties antinuclear poem 'Your Attention Please') to Robert Minhinnick's stunning 'Twenty-Five Laments For Iraq' via 'Three Ways To A Silk Shirt' (Pamela Gillilan), 'Five Sketches' (Robert Wells), and 'Eight Ways Of Looking At Lakes' (Matthew Caley).

Preferences? George Szirtes' 'Backwaters: Norfolk Fields', a sonnet sequence where timbre and execution are just about faultless; John Burnside's 'The Asylum Dance' – assured, perfectly paced; Mark Halliday's witty '*Whang* Editorial Policy'; Jackie Kay's dental extravaganza 'Crown and Country'; and Roger McGough's 'The Way Things Are': each has above-average immediacy and hardly wastes a word. The last-named deserves special mention in that language is used surreally without imploding as gobbledegook, demonstrating a fertile rather than a febrile imagination: "Even telescopes, like the rest of us, grow bored"; "though your shadow is shortening / it does not mean you are growing smaller"; "Moonbeams sadly, will not survive in a jar"; "The thrill of being a shower curtain will soon pall".... The poem is an exercise in Dadaism, the nihilistic artistic movement founded on irrationality, incongruity, and irreverence towards accepted aesthetic criteria. All except nihilism (especially when it is revolutionary and destructive) can be life-enhancing and should be more readily celebrated.

Underachievers? Sophie Hannah's 'Next Door Despised' is nonsense verse which sounds as if it expects to be taken seriously; Michael Hofmann's 'Last Walk' falters when he lists images in the hope that their whole will exceed the sum of their parts; Bernard O'Donoghue's 'Hermes' concludes "Christmas is the worst time of all / For the person living on their own", providing a dud end to a dud poem; Peter Porter's 'To My Grandaughters [sic]

Sweeping Spelsbury Church' has content too tightly yoked to form (nonetheless, it's good to see a poet wrestling with a fixed rhyme-scheme and the demands of craftsmanship); Adam Thorpe's 'Pickings' is an unconvincing attempt in which monosyllables predominate; Jeffrey Wainwright's 'The Humane House' is simply prolix; and Robert Wells' 'Five Sketches' left me cold.

Neither good nor bad but inhabiting his own peculiar locale lurks Andrew Motion, whose novelistic 'Serenade' buttonholes us amiably by way of "arsehole", "cunt", "shit", and "piss". One wonders whether the laureateship will blunt his style.

You can order this book POST-FREE from the PBS at £7.95. See p.94 for details.

Taking a Break

by Neil Powell

ADAM THORPE

From the Neanderthal

Cape, £8.00
ISBN 0 224 03971 7

GILLIAN CLARKE

Five Fields

Carcanet, £6.95
ISBN 1 85754 401 3

HERBERT LOMAS

A Useless Passion

London Magazine Editions, £7.95
ISBN see below

BLAKE MORRISON

Selected Poems

Granta, £8.99
ISBN 1 86207 291 4

ADAM THORPE'S REMARKABLE new collection (his first since 1990, though in the meantime he's published three novels) offers compelling evidence in favour of taking a break. Perhaps more writers should try it – Hardy, after all, re-emerged as an infinitely stronger poet after his novel-writing years – though of course the chances are that Thorpe has been accumulating these poems steadily and, anyway, a nine-year gap between volumes is the approved Larkinesque interval.

Nevertheless, it's not fanciful to suggest that in this case writing fiction has benefited the poet in two complementary ways: on the one hand, it's made him far less nervous than many of his drab-voiced contemporaries about poetry's particular resources; on the other, it's given him the confidence to go for prosaic, even bathetic statement when this happens to suit his purpose. The first of these characteristics erupts splendidly in the opening poem, 'Against', with its infectious delight in alliteration and rhyme – "scoop and shave the grain / to serviceable lightness, take the rein" – while 'Tending the Stove', a couple of pages on, a poem which manages to contain non-standard usages of both "fell" and "felloe" within half a dozen lines, is clearly the work of a writer unashamedly relishing choiceness of language. The second provides effects as daring as this opening stanza from 'Playground Accident', where the utterly collapsed final line articulates dull disbelief:

> My son's forehead's snickered across
> yet again by thread; like tiny flies
> the stitches have settled for days, but a year
> and a half is the scar's reign,
> according to the doctor.

This is one of several occasions on which the poet's children are called upon to illustrate the oddness or cussedness of the world: another high-risk strategy, yet Thorpe employs it to achieve acuteness rather than just cuteness. One lovely poem has him trying to explain to his son why our footprints are always behind us (or, as the child puts it, "Footprints aren't ever where you haven't been'd") and why his seven-week-old daughter can't be expected to make any of her own; another finds him coping with a (different or older) daughter's conviction that the man on a wayside crucifix has fallen in the water and been hung up to dry, before deciding that this childish heresy is after all an instance of "the world made mad in the right way".

The other recurring strand in *From the*

Neanderthal is broadly archeological, and here the occupational hazard is that the poems may remain a bit notebooky and untransformed: there are hints of this in 'Fossil' and in the concluding sequence, but 'Pickings' is a huge success, its monosyllables and bits and pieces of rhyme neatly matching the random finds of excavation: "keys stuck in rust's lock, // lots of bits of pot, / jabs in glass for goats // and knobs for doors long shut / from hands...". In a very different tonal register, Thorpe can cope with the chillingly demotic (the ex-soldier in 'Windows' is a grim instance) but he knows just when to stop. Elsewhere, the collection is peppered with phrases I'd noted for possible quotation, such as "the backs of birds actually in flight" seen from the Big Wheel and "Time's wedded to what it wields" from 'Anniversary'. In short, this is an extraordinarily impressive book.

Gillian Clarke

Taking a break, in a rather different sense, is at the heart of Gillian Clarke's latest collection too. In 1997 she undertook a residency at the Bridgewater Hall, Manchester – culture-shock enough, one might think, for a poet so closely identified with Welsh rural life, but all the more so since this was a city only slowly recovering from the IRA bomb in 1996 which devastated its centre (including the offices of her publisher). *Five Fields* opens, however, with poems about the subjects with which she is most closely identified, farming and family life in Wales. These have a consistent feeling of lived-in authenticity, especially when the two intermingle and disrupt each other: in 'A Difficult Birth, Easter 1998', for instance, the finely exact account of an old ewe's lambing gains an additional validating resonance from its juxtaposition with the postponed "quiet supper and bottle of wine / we'd planned, to celebrate if the news is good"; the awaited "news" is that of the "Irish peace deal", another difficult birth, rather than that from the farm which, by the end of the poem, has supplanted it. That sort of multi-layering – which seems in the simplest and most honourable way "true to life" – recurs in a different, equally striking context in 'Unpacking the Angel'; for among the Christmas decorations stored in the loft and annually rediscovered are some which prompt beautifully evoked family memories and others with altogether more surprising associations:

From the Christmas fair on the Küfurstendam
two crystal drops, rousing from the drafts
that stir the tree the whine of air-raids,
the church in flame, stained glass bursting.
And the Berlin angel, whose sleeves still bear
a trace of concrete from the broken wall.

If the two Manchester sequences at the heart of the book – 'The City' and 'Concerto' – seem by comparison a touch effortful, it's because they necessarily cut away from the complexities of allegiances and rootedness which are Gillian Clarke's abiding themes: the first especially, in its dutiful naming of places, declares its status as a commissioned poem too insistently. But her account of the bomb and its aftermath is beautifully controlled. It would take a churlish reader to begrudge her the contrast between the publisher's office on that Saturday morning, "where poetry's quiet, compressed in the book's pages / and phones and computers are taking the day off", and the scene seconds later:

On the palm of the ledge outside the publisher's
　　　　　　　　　　　　　　　　　　　　　window
in the Corn Exchange is clutch of broken eggs,
Fledglings blown away twig-limbed and goggle-eyed.

Herbert Lomas

More sequences, three of them this time, make up Herbert Lomas's substantial latest collection. This is really two very different short books: the first part, 'Called to the Colours', is a "minor historical narrative" of the author's army life between 1943 and 1946; the remaining sections both relate to the death of his second wife, Mary, in 1994. The chronological distance is, as one might expect, more than equalled by a startling disparity of tone.

Tone, as so often with Lomas (and not in a wholly disadvantageous way), is the problem: he's a writer who can move from colloquial chumminess to stately pomposity in an instant, which for the reader may be effectively disconcerting or just confusing. The blurb describes 'Called to the Colours' as a "wartime sequence", a phrase which ordinarily means "a sequence written in wartime", and indeed the poems have from the very start a brash immediacy: "'Yer eyes are like pissoles in the snow'. / Sergeant Birkett fixes us / with a seagull stare". Yet is this the actual voice of the nineteen-year-old Lomas in 1943 or is it a reconstruction? A bit of both, I'd guess, but the point is worth worrying about precisely because the tone of a young man's actual observations on service life – which, if authentic, ought to be slotted retrospectively into place in anthologies of Second World War writing – might be expected to differ from the oldish man's recollections. As it is, "young" Lomas manages to combine appropriate naivety with notable perceptions (it doesn't take him long, listening to Corporal Cosgrove and others, to recognise that in matters of sex, as in so much else, bravado and experience tend to occur in inverse proportions); and these diary-like jottings, lightly and benignly sketched, certainly add convincing anecdotal details to material familiar from other writers – the transit camp and troopship poems, for instance, inevitably recall Roy Fuller's on identical subjects and deserve to stand beside them.

The spare, movingly direct poems of bereavement, 'Death of a Horsewoman', are fleetingly troubled by a different sort of tonal problem: it's there in lines such as "I listen for a horse neighing far off, / your usual sign, but nothing comes", where Lomas's subdued diction seems briefly at odds with ghostly echoes from Yeats (the imagined horse, the self-dramatising present tense). It's a small blemish, though, and these poems work best – like Gillian Clarke's – when their larger themes collide with domestic detail:

> I take the glass you had engraved
> with HL and pour myself a whisky.
> Since you went, I celebrate our
> second marriage, and I'm becoming
> newly acquainted with us all.

Those carefully suspended opening lines of 'Glass Darkly' lead to a summoning of dead friends, both met and unmet ("Sibelius is here, sharing my whisky"), in a quietly effective act of remembrance.

With *A Useless Passion* Lomas returns to his former publisher, the admirable London Magazine Editions. Though earlier LM books were very elegant things, this one has been rather messily if readably typeset; more seriously, since it lacks both ISBN and barcode, many bookshops will be unable to stock or order it, which is perhaps taking dogged independence to an unhelpful extreme. Interested readers might be best advised to write to LM at 30 Thurloe Place, London SW7 2HQ.

Blake Morrison

I returned to Blake Morrison's poems in much the same spirit as Benjamin Britten used periodically to revisit the works of Brahms: to see whether they could really be as dreadful as I remembered. Britten, finding his worst fears confirmed, was – I now think – uncharacteristically wrong; I wish I had been too. And yet the matter isn't quite straightforward, for Morrison's first collection, *Dark Glasses* (1984), was a fairly impressive affair which contained at least one outstanding poem – a supple, poignant little narrative piece called 'Grange Boy', which teasingly declined quite to unravel its central enigma ("English, we hoard our secrets to the end"). Then came *The Ballad of the Yorkshire Ripper* (1987), centred upon a poem which Morrison probably shouldn't have written; or, once written, shouldn't have published; or, once published, shouldn't have reprinted in this *Selected Poems*. Any writer could have made the first two errors of judgement; the third is inexcusable.

Nor, as it happens, was that the only snag with *The Ballad of the Yorkshire Ripper*: there were other pieces (such as the thankfully discarded 'Night Mail' and the retained 'On Sizewell Beach') which made one wonder whether Morrison had any idea at all of the differences between poetry and prose, any sense of rhythm or cadence, any enjoyment of language: in fact, much of the book signalled Morrison's emerging vocation as a writer of journalistic prose with an interest in criminality. Now, this new volume, which "includes previously unpublished poems", suggests that Morrison the poet is alive and well; and chief among these newly-collected pieces (heftily disguised by a scrambled order which puts some earlier and better poems strategically near the end) is a sequence called 'Madrigalia'. Here's a fair sample:

> The print of soles across the bathroom floor:
> finding them, I felt like Crusoe, and stooped
> to test their warmth and wetness, then rose
> to follow where they led, not caring that
> I knew the end already, as if she were
> a stranger, this woman meeting my eyes
> in the dressing-table mirror

The first line is verse, the rest prose; the sentence continues for a further six shapeless lines. There's nothing particularly wrong with such writing, apart from the fact that it isn't poetry. The best advice might be to take a break.

You can order these books POST-FREE from the PBS. See p.94 for details.

Memory, Patience and Dissipation

by Elaine Feinstein

In the Grip of Strange Thoughts: Russian Poetry in a New Era
Ed. J. Kates
Bloodaxe, £12.95
ISBN 1 85224 478 X

SOME TIME IN 1997, just before the collapse of the rouble, I was taken to the Cafe Idiot on the Moyka in St Petersburg by a Director of Studies in Economics. When I inquired about the latest poets to surface in the New Russia, he was impatient with me. The Russian passion for poetry had little place in a lively, entrepreneurial society, he assured me. On the same visit, Alexander Kushner, the most distinguished poet in St Petersburg, and the indomitable Yunna Morits in Moscow, confirmed gloomily that sales of poetry had shrunk to almost Anglo Saxon levels. Neither seemed much excited by an emerging avant garde.

So I turned to this book with curiosity. I wasn't entirely surprised to find that the first hundred pages had been drawn from a pantheon already in place in the seventies. The title itself is taken from a song of Bulat Okudzhava, celebrated for more than 25 years before the Soviet Union collapsed.

More disappointingly, some poets were represented by familiar poems, often frequently translated ones. Bella Akhmadulina's 'Fever', for instance, had been translated by several hands including my own as long ago as '76; while Irina Ratushinskaya has lived in London for many years, celebrated for her courageous anti-Soviet stance, and her moving camp memoir *Grey is the Colour of Hope*.

That said, there is much to enjoy in this anthology, and the editor has found some remarkable voices from an older generation which amply deserved to be recovered from neglect: Inna Lisnianskaya, for instance, first published by Tvardovsky in Novy Mir in 1957. She resigned from the Writers Union in protest against political interference with the unofficial magazine *Metropol*.

Unlike more prominent writers such as Vosnesensky and Akhmadulina who were also involved, Lisnianskaya's work went unpublished for nearly twenty years. So she writes

> Spring is in full bloom: the time has come
> For the spirit to be free,
> And I can hear open speech from the streets
> But I am already an old woman...

Evgeny Rein, too, one of the circle of young poets around Akhmatova, went largely unpublished until 1979. Since then, and particularly since the collapse of the Soviet system, he has published 10 volumes of poetry and was awarded the State Prize for poetry in 1997. Rein can work without rhyme, as in a particularly moving poem dedicated to the memory of his nanny Tanya.

> Today the fragrance of September fills the air.
> It smells of dust and apples
> and paint from the cemetery fences

His thoughts return to his own asthmatic childhood, his fear of suffocation, and his nanny's advice:

> What we need in this life:
> first a long memory and secondly,
> patience and Russian dissipation

He concludes by invoking the spirit of Louis Armstrong as the Black archangel who will sound the trumpet call over a land "Russian, Jewish and American".

The youngest poets in this anthology were born in the forties, and among them Elena Schwartz, Olga Sedakova and Tatiana Bek stand out. All of them deserve to be better known here. When I read Elena Schwartz's *Paradise* some years ago I found her powerfully disturbing, with a violence of imagery which makes Sylvia Plath sound measured in comparison.

> Your skin is leprous; you're pink and blistered
> as a child inundated in scalding soup.

Olga Sedakova, in contrast, is a lyrical inheritor of that great Russian tradition of women's poetry which Yunna Morits refers to ironically as being measured in "Akhmatsvets". One poem, which takes off from a line of Keats, is impressively translated here by Catriona Kelly:

REVIEWS

The poetry of earth can never die.
Here in the North when once the first snow falls,
the grasshopper is still, but blizzards start to whirl
and crickets start to strum like men gone blind.

As this is a bilingual edition, you can make out Sedakova's elegant simplicity of rhyme and pace. Tatyana Bek, among the freshest voices of the same generation, offers fewer problems for her translator, since her appeal lies in the sudden, startling signs that give her strength like "the poppies turning red / with their black ink hearts".

All anthologies have arbitrary features, and no doubt it was right to leave out Yevtushenko and Voznesensky, whose travels in the West during the Soviet years contributed to the waning enthusiasm for their poetry at home. More dubious was the decision to exclude poets who died before 1990, so that there is nothing from two poet singers, Vysotsky and Galich – both edgier and more subversive than Okudzhava – or the fine poet Boris

You can order this book POST-FREE from the PBS at £12.95. See p.94 for details.

From My Province

by Gillian Allnutt

MAXINE KUMIN

Selected Poems 1960–1990

Norton, £10.95
ISBN 0 393 31836 2

KUMIN IMAGINES SHOPPING in the market in Ferney (France, over the border from Geneva) with the ghost of Voltaire:

> Fingering the fringy cornucopias
> of black chanterelles
> (*les trompettes de la mort*) he quotes
> himself: *qui veut voir une ombre?*
> I've read that in the Besterman
> biography.
> ('Shopping in Ferney with Voltaire')

There's a humorous, straightforward acknowledgement of sources which is typical of Kumin's work. In 'On Being Asked to Write a Poem for the Centenary of the Civil War' she sketches the story of her great-grandfather's life: "an escaped conscript / blasted out of Europe in 1848", he "sailed in at Baltimore / a Jew, and poor", set himself up as a tailor in Virginia and grew rich "stitching uniforms for the Confederates". "Good friend", she asks, "from my province what is there to say?".

There is a great deal to say, it seems. Novelist, short story writer, essayist and children's author (she collaborated on two books for children with Anne Sexton), Kumin has been prolific. This selection includes work from nine poetry collections

published before 1990 and runs to nearly three hundred pages. I believe she would have been better served as a poet here with a slimmer selection from a British publisher with an introduction or even just an informative back cover blurb aimed at the British market. In a world where it's already so hard to keep up with reading, such a fat book from a relatively "unmapped" poet is likely to be laid aside.

She was born in Philadelphia in 1925, of Jewish/German/Central European ancestry. She lives on a farm in New Hampshire, raising horses. She has three grown-up children. She was a close friend of Anne Sexton. She had a neighbour named Henry Manley. She writes about all these things and her New Hampshire habitat and bears and, in the later collections, threatened animal species, a threatened earth. Like other confessional poets, she centres her work in herself and the "dailiness" of her life, moving outwards from these in time and space, with honesty and humour. Some of my favourite poems are from *Up Country*, a quiet celebration of her rural New England life, which was awarded the Pulitzer Prize in 1973. Among these, the poem I like best is, paradoxically, one that points to the faint possibility of being rooted in something more abiding than the personal self:

> The doors of my house are held open by stones
> and to see the tame herd of them hump their
>   backbones
>
> as cumbrous as bears across the pasture in
> an allday rain is to believe for an afternoon
>
> of objects that waver and blur
> in some dark obedient order.
>   ('Stones')

Kumin is often deceptively simple – so much so,

I'd say she does herself a disservice. If I hadn't been reading to review, I might have missed the subtleties of syntax, the narrative skill and the precision, care and confidence with which she chooses her words.

A number of poems deal with the progress of her love in the aftermath of Anne Sexton's suicide in 1974, when both poets were in their forties. By the time she is interviewed by Sexton's biographer, she can write:

> Soon I will be sixty.
> How it was with you now
> hardly more vivid than how
> it is without you, I carry
> the sheer weight of the telling
> like a large infant, on one hip.
> ('Apostrophe to a Dead Friend')

Always she describes their friendship as a womanly thing, and yet, in 'On Being Asked to Write a Poem in Memory of Anne Sexton', she comes up with the image of the elk's antlers, grown anew each year – and "destined to ossify", as were both the pain in Sexton's life as it became poetry and the life as it became (and becomes) the literary reputation.

Though she notes more than once, and with pleasure, the "androgyny" of later life, Kumin always writes as a woman. A long poem towards the end of the selection weaves together the lives of her biological mother, a "literary mother", Marianne Moore, and herself, creating a kind of "herstory" of America in the Twentieth Century and recording a specifically female experience of the relationship between public and private life. Kumin concludes 'Marianne, My Mother, and Me' with this:

> I claim them both as mine
> whose lives began in a gentler time and place...
>
> before man split the atom, thrust the jet,
> procured the laser, shot himself through space,
> both shapers of my alphabet.

You can order this book POST-FREE from the PBS at £10.95. See p.94 for details.

Something to Say

By Kwame Dawes

MARCIA DOUGLAS
Electricity Comes to Cocoa Bottom
Peepal Tree, £6.99
ISBN 1 900715 28 7

ISHMAEL FIIFI ANNOBIL
Seven Horn Elegy
Totem, £6.99
ISBN 1 899151 00 1

JACK MAPANJE
Skipping Without Ropes
Bloodaxe, £6.95
ISBN 1 85224412 7

THESE THREE NEW collections of poetry represent important stages in the career of three very engaging voices in poetry that can be said to have emerged from Africa and its Diaspora. Two are debut collections and the third is perhaps one of the last summations of a terrible and harrowing experience that has ultimately brought forth a poetic work that brings an uneasy peace. Two of the poets, Fiifi Annobil and Jack Mapanje, are relatively recent African transplants to the United Kingdom – exiles, if you will. Marcia Douglas is a Jamaican living in North Carolina and writing about Jamaica with a predictable sense of nostalgia, but a more surprising quality of irony and complex reflection. I am trying to connect these writers through the details of their biographies, but they are as different in personal histories as they are in their poetic inclinations. A review of the three must constitute a celebration of variety and if there is a common instinct that they share, it is one that most poets share – the pleasure in relishing the possibilities of words placed side by side, and a belief in the grace to be found in story telling.

Marcia Douglas
Marcia Douglas's *Electricity Come to Cocoa Bottom* won a recommendation from the Poetry Book Society, and they did so praising the work for it for Douglas' capacity to discover poetic meaning in a range of emotional experiences. The poems trace a woman's journey across the Caribbean Sea and deep into the American world. She is really charting a

journey that has been taken by more and more Jamaicans in the last twenty years. The migratory patterns are no longer the ones that marked the movement of the earlier Caribbean writers who found their Mecca in England. America is where Douglas and a host of other Caribbean poets have found their exile and theirs is not an exile complicated by the miasma of colonialism. Now, the dialogue is between an equally unsettling imperialism: the meaning of America in the 1970s and 1980s in the Caribbean. The Caribbean exile in America is there for very useful reasons – to go to school, to get a good job, to become a part of a larger immigrant society that thrives in America. Home, therefore has the kind of resonance that it did not have for the boat-travelers of the fifties and the sixties. Douglas's poetry reminds us constantly that "home" is not far away. That returning "home" is quite easy to do. Thus the politics of home and being away from home are subsumed by a quest to create a history that is distinctive and that is, ultimately affirming. "Home" is therefore not competing for relevance and meaning, it is merely demanding that it become a part of the imaginative landscape of this writer.

Douglas's poems about home are poems that remind us a great deal of two other Jamaican poets: Lorna Goodison and Olive Senior. Douglas has read these two women and she shows a confidence about the value of incantation and the naming of places and objects that are connected to the language and landscape of the country that has come to mark Lorna Goodison's poetry. From Senior, one gets a willingness to create a tenuous distance between the poet and the narrative, a distance enacted by formal variations and the posture of memory. Douglas is most convincing when she handles matters of emotional depth and complexity. Her instinct is not to mask but to unmask and to try and spread out the details of loss, fear, and the tenderness of love. There is something refreshing about that open-handed telling. The effect of her dogged belief in the truth of love, of lasting love between people, for instance, is to make believers of the readers. We travel with her willingly.

Douglas's line is always tidy but never so tidy that it seems affected. Indeed there are stretches of her poems that seem determined to create a prosaic casualness. But the suddenly arrival of an image or the cleverness of a line-break reminds us quickly that a careful act of craft is taking place before us.

Here is one of the most moving poems in the collection:

> When Daddy got baptised in Yallahs River he rose
> up speaking – Oh-shali-waa-shali-mahi-wa.
> His eyes shut tight as a newborn's, someone wrapped
> him in a white sheet and led him out to the water.
> The brethren clapping and singing redemption, the
> white-wings flew

This is poetry that has mastered the genius of the line-break and that has captured the remarkable rituals of language in this narrative of birth. Douglas' poetry is always tidy, always carefully balanced and always focused on exploring detail.

Since I fully expect Douglas, who also writes novels, to write more poetry, I expect that this collection will constitute one of the ground-clearing moments in her career that we will return to again and again in the future.

Ishmael Fiifi Annobil

There is nothing in Fiifi Annobil's collection, *Seven Horn Elegy* that suggests that this is a first collection. There is a reason for this. Annobil has been writing for over twenty years at a sustained and impressive level. He began as a prodigy among the avant-garde surreal and experimental poets of Accra, Ghana in the late seventies. Their influence is still there in his poems that are always tersely constructed. Annobil's verse arrives at unquestionable brilliance because of the devotion that he has to making every image and every idea expressed fresh and distinctive. There is then, something quite extraordinary about the way his poems establish a rich discourse between the ideologies and experiences of several very different worlds in which he has lived. There is a startling modernity to his line, his imagery and his constant desire to create surprise by clashing images: "Garland of hollies;.." is how he begins his seemingly benign Christmas poem "Yule-Log." But all predictability is shot in the next several lines:

> Floating mid-earth, centred
> By the storm's eye;
>
> A muler, dragged out
> Of a wilderness,
> Trailed by cornucopia
> Of thorns:

REVIEWS

Those last two lines with their suggestion of sacrifice and betrayal, of pain and torture are nicely reflective of the manner in which Annobil makes the very landscape he draws, a body, a subject of suffering:

> The earth is thus
> Impaled, waiting for the wind to clear, The cock-crows are already done;
>
> The supplications are passionate,
> Frenzied in a foetal yearning.

Annobil takes his religion clean and sharp and this quality of contained sentiment, of restraint and the heady intelligence of complex vocabulary and coined phrase is trade mark Annobil. You can tell he relishes the sound of words. You can't help but admire a poet who argues in his poems that the poet's art is tragically empty in language and formal care that belies the very testimony he is giving:

> A trapped dove
> Lain on its side
> In the snow.
>
> Passers-by pluck a feather
> Or two for doffed hats.
>
> Dequilled stump; a frozen
> Norm.
>
> Bearer of an ill-fated
> Message

The title poem of the series shows that Annobil has located his influences not only in the most obvious places (you can smell the minimalism of Japanese forms and a certain Pound-like toughness of line and a 19th century French symbolism in much of the verse collected here) but in the rich heritage of language and culture that is his. "Seven Horn Elegy" is a poem for his father – a poem framed by the Akan dirge sang at the burial of a great leader. Annobil writes in Ga and in Akan. He maintains the cadence of the traditional praise poet in the poem:

> And I too have come to
> Undress the belaboured litanies
> Of gilded apostasy, the fuming
> Censers of apostolic
> Imposters
> That defile the faucet
> Our angels sip from.

The surrealism of his other poems is not lost, but now the rhetoric is captured in the declamatory tones of the praise singer. This is good poetry. Exciting poetry. Annobil is an exciting poet not because of his noble examinations of the plight of Africans or the plight of the poor, or his unabashed celebration of a world in which people from different races can come together through an engagement in language and plain neighbourliness, but because his verse is such a finely wrought entity. It is a study in editorial ruthlessness and a refined instinct for the rightly turned image.

Jack Mapanje

Jack Mapanje's latest collection, *Skipping Without Ropes* introduces a number of problems that will constantly haunt poets and lovers of poetry. Many poets would die (an unfortunate choice of words but we will leave it alone) for the kind of subject that Mapanje has to work with. He was imprisoned unfairly by a brutish political regime in Malawi. He lived to write about it. I say a lot of poets would like to have such material to work with but I may be wrong. Indeed in the last few months my conversation with several poets suggests to me that the business of wanting to say something in a poem is the worst place to start making a poem. This is not really their idea. Auden went on about this some years ago. For him the poet was the one who wanted to play with words. Good. But what was the person who had something to say? Clearly not the poet. But we would surely have to eliminate far too many poets if the weight of experience and the desire to articulate such experience was not a burning drive in the making of the poems. Mapanje has a story to tell and it is a harrowing story of betrayals and torture and a story about death and the struggle to reconcile the pains of imprisonment with the routines of normal life. And it is a true story about his imprisonment in Malawi without trial or charge by the regime of Hastings Banda. I would like to say that regardless of what the subject of these poems was, I would still be deeply engrossed in the language and the form of the poems for their own sake. But I can't. And that is not a criticism. I am impressed and moved by the experiences that Mapanje describes and the telling of them, in many ways, sells the collection for me. When a poet experiences, a poet wants to write experience. The poet must not be sent to a memoir editor for the poet writes in poetry, tells in poetry, retrieves in poetry. The poet must tell his or her story in poetry. This is poetry:

> Our answers splash down David Livingstone's
> cataracts,
> Surfing past the baobab trees of our Kasisi
> Traditional
> Authority, nibs spill out ink as bounteously as
> bee-eater
> Droppings adorn Bishop Mackenzie's grave stone!

And there is much more of this in the collection. But it does weigh heavily on the reader, this collection. Image after image, story after story of the hardships of prison, of the terrible price paid for injustice and corruption in totalitarian regimes eventually slow the reader down. You start to read the volume in small bites, at shorter sittings because the narrative is too disturbing. There are times, in places like this, that you suspect that the verse has left the idea of playing with language and turned to something akin to a ramble – a strangely calculated ramble that could easily be called prose:

> But as the check-point boss flicks through my Wad
> of T-shirts, a soldier rushes in, swinging AK47,
> bringing an urgent message from his boss, "Sorry,
> Bwana, but that truck has bandits with
>
> Two AK47s, one's loaded, come, rescue, quick".

Here you wonder if, given more time to discover the distilled terror of that moment, Mapanje could not have written a shorter, more terrifying poem. But you are still carried by the story and you are still impressed by the righteousness of the cause and you are still forced to ask hard questions about the relative value of poetry. One can't help but suspect that those who are comfortable with the notion of making poems purely for the pleasure of words are those who have nothing to say. But that is sheer arrogance, a quality that none of the three poets I have talked about here appear to share. They do share, however, a desire to speak of experience with a sense of the world that offers a place for the poet.

You can order these books POST-FREE from the PBS. See p.94 for details.

RICHARD KELL
HEISENBERG IN COPENHAGEN

"Not nature in itself, but nature
exposed to our method of questioning".
Did that disturb you, or were you glad
some truth would outreach for ever
the equations and the measuring rod?
I'd like to have been there, that blue midnight,
when you strolled on the promenade
with Pauli, and spoke of the soul and Pascal's "fire" –
mysteries presupposed
by the lovely patterns they elude –
and a liner gliding past, "its bright lights
fabulous and unreal", made
you think about intentions, formative power,
a consciousness you couldn't quite call God.

ANNE GRAY
14 WAYS OF BEING IN PRAGUE

The couple from Venezuela are in Copenhagen
in the morning. They tell me they are lonely.
Three Muslim women have trapped the porter.

They tell him there are gangsters in the taxis.
The man from Afghanistan tells me he is from
a pure country. He eats heavy bread

with caraway seeds. I want a pancake
stuffed with figs and limp with cream.
The waiter almost smiles when he brings it.

The pianist gives us 'Strangers in the Night'
then all the songs from *My Fair Lady* –
though everything he starts ends

unexpectedly. The girl in blue sequins
is waiting for a friend. She tells the Maitre
she's not working. The room is lit by

falling beads of glass. The pianist reaches
for Rachmaninov, or is it Grieg?
He's drinking Pivo and he's smoking.

When I phoned, she told me you were sleeping.
I've started taking sugar in my tea.
A man swallows swords in Old Town Square.

I hate it, but I watch him. It gets dark early
in this exquisite city. I watch the maid
fold eiderdowns in linen for my bed.

JANE HOLLAND
IN PRAISE OF CANNABIS

for Will

How do I love thee? Mainly by inhaling thee
through a tube of ultra-thin rolling paper
finely laced with tobacco, but also
by licking my fingers after crumbling the block
or discovering stray skunk on the rug
weeks later, when I've promised myself
no more, and an end to all that
yet the smell comes back, like a punch
in the throat, until there's nothing
you can do but go out and score,
because there are smokers and then
there are puffers, and even when you're clear,
the gear wins, hands down. It's the best prison
in the world, and after a while, all you get is
slightly toasted, and you long for those days
when the animal hit you between the eyes
and your knees refused to move, tingling
with a not unpleasant electric shock,
but now you'd need a monster party spliff
to achieve that sort of damage, and you must
stay straight or you can't keep rolling.
In spite of this, caning is a useful pursuit
for the socially adventurous: you meet all sorts
of interesting dealers and people who worship
animal spirits or use oriental bongs
they picked up in a den in Amsterdam.
But at the end of the day, when most
sane people are tucked up in bed, it's just you
and the beast, and she's so beautiful,
the smoke-haze is nectar, and you drift,
not sleepy, not thinking, but definitely there
where everything is manageable, sorted.

CARMINE STARNINO
1955

The year Albert Einstein dies my mother is taught
To balance a jar of water on her head. She's great
At math, so when she dunks the jar into the well
I have her count each gulp as the clay belly grows

Heavy in her hands. The year a UK team conquers
The Kanchenjunga in the Himalayas, the highest
Unclimbed peak, the village boys take a tippy-toe
Peek over the stone wall behind her, using a pile

Of stones to stand on. My mother lifts out the jar,
Places it on the ledge, and while the BBC reveals
The world's first color TV, she pinches two opposite
Corners of a white handkerchief, skipping-ropes it

Into a long finger which she coils around the top
Of her head as a cushion. Not exactly Marilyn Monroe
Over a subway grating, her skirt huffing open
In an uprush of air, but for the boys, enough to exceed

The imagination's 200 mph limit, like the record
Donald Campbell broke in his turbo-jet hydroplane
Bluebird. Yardbird? That's right, Charlie Parker
Died too. I'd love to introduce some bebop into this,

Trumpet and saxophone, a crazy tune each boy
Improvises in his heart, as my mother crowns herself
With the jar, and climbs the hill home, keeping
Level the concupiscence in their bodies, the water.

KEVIN MURRAY
GETTING ON

You should understand I no longer scan
new calendars, guessing at my end-day.
No future in that

I've schooled myself to discard old things –
worn chairs, shirts, shoes – all quite forgotten
within a month or so.

Once past the drowning panic I sleep well
enough, casting no-one older than twenty
in my humid dreams.

Never trust the winter trees. They mime decline,
infect us with their gloom, then bounce back
in smug green.

Come clear nights I cheer for the new moon
in its growing, find things to do indoors
as it wanes.

By and large I'm easy within this shifting present
despite small shocks, like drawing the last tissue
from that box.

REVIEWS

Two Prophets

DENNIS O'DRISCOLL ON TWO RADICAL, POLITICIZED POETS

ALLEN GINSBERG

**Death & Fame:
Poems 1993–1997**

Penguin, £7.99
ISBN 0 14 118184 2

ADRIENNE RICH

**Midnight Salvage:
Poems 1995–1998**

Norton, £14.95
ISBN 0 393 04682 6

HE WAS BORN in 1926. She was born in 1929. Allen Ginsberg's Jewish father was a teacher who also published poetry. Adrienne Rich's Jewish father was a scientist and "amateur poet". Both Ginsberg and Rich began as formalists. Both were strongly influenced by many of the same poets, from William Blake to William Carlos Williams. Both protested vehemently against the Vietnam War and were tireless campaigners for social justice. Both spoke up for sexual emancipation – she as feminist and lesbian, he as libertarian and homosexual. The 1974 National Book Award was shared between them.

Ginsberg's rhetoric may be louder and gaudier than Rich's; yet, by giving voice to voiceless women, she lays claim to an even more far-reaching agenda than his. In a 1980 interview, she commented that "It would interest me if I saw men... really being able to take the risks that women are taking, have taken, not just on our own behalf but on behalf of every movement against oppression, through all history". The "Please Do Not Disturb" sign, famously suspended by Ginsberg from his penis at a party, flashed exactly the opposite message to what feminists like Rich had in mind. While Ginsberg gave credit to President Clinton for raising the question of gay membership of the US armed forces, Rich contended that the "very institution of the military itself" was the real issue.

Allen Ginsberg's career as a poet ended in the early hours of March 30th 1997, a week before his death, when he penned the list entitled 'Things I'll Not Do (Nostalgias)', the final poem in *Death & Fame*. His list begins with Albania and Bulgaria – among the few places on the globe where he had failed, in seventy hectic years of life, to leave his sandal prints. For a man who proclaimed that "Fossil Fuels retard the planet", he did more than his share – abetted by Volkswagen campers and international airlines – to accelerate its retardation. As befitted an inveterate *New York Times* reader, Ginsberg reacted spontaneously in verse to day-to-day events and sometimes merely sounded like a cranky correspondent to the Letters page. The evils of the World Bank, the plight of the homeless, the duplicity of Senator Jesse Helms "the Moralist King" all receive attention in his farewell collection.

The validity of Ginsberg's viewpoint is rarely in doubt (always allowing for rhetorical hyperbole, especially where the woes of America are concerned); but when the poetical response is as predictable as the polemical one, his repeated outrage achieves nothing more productive than tedium. A poem like 'Newt Gingrich Declares War on "McGovernik Counterculture"' already looks as dated and yellow as a 1995 newspaper cutting. It is sad to find Ginsberg in the year of his death squandering his considerable talent on 'Virtual Impunity Blues', a protest poem aimed at the old reliables (President, Pope, FBI, CIA) which is effective neither as protest nor as poetry. There is much in *Death & Fame* which would amuse and entertain in performance – and Ginsberg was a feisty, charismatic, rousing performer. On the less mesmerising page, however, his "First thought, best thought" approach to writing can evoke a "First reading, last reading" reproach from his readership. A number of the poems are proof that fame – with the fawning indulgence it brings – can spell death for the self-critical faculty. Some poems in *Death & Fame* are platitudes masquerading as prophecies; others would bring a rash of blushes even to the cheeks of a McGonagall:

I'll be leaving for retreat,
Where they make me salt-free meat
along with Gelek Rinpoche
Who's got ailments same as me,

in Michigan Camp Copneconic
Where I'll room with Mr. Harmonic...

Ginsberg's exuberance and humour are more winning in 'C'mon Pigs of Western Civilization Eat More Grease' where he lards his high calorie descriptions of fatty foods until laughter and disgust are simultaneously provoked. Finally – a true disciple of Blake – he sees a world in a grain of fat:

> ...Western cuisine rich in protein
> cancer heart attack
>   hypertension sweat
>   bloated liver & spleen
>   megaly
> Diabetes & stroke –
>   monuments to carnivorous
>   civilizations
>   presently murdering
>   Belfast
>   Bosnia Cypress (sic)
>   Ngorno Karabach
>   Georgia...

Quieter successes in *Death & Fame* include the elegies for youth ('"You know what I'm saying?"', 'Popular Tunes'). Old enough to qualify for senior citizen discount at Alfalfa's Healthfoods, Ginsberg touchingly recalls the songs of his boyhood "echoing thru Time's skull as my beard's / turned white"; or he meets, fifty years later at a school reunion ("retired, wife on his arm"), somebody whose beauty once left him "dumbstruck". The drugs Ginsberg takes are no longer illicit or hallucinogenic but rather prescription medicines for high blood pressure and heart complaints. With the explicitness of a poet who eagerly adopted Whitman's "suggestions for candor, spontaneity, openness, frankness", Ginsberg spares the reader no detail of his bodily functions and this collection displays marked coprophiliac tendencies. He brings to the "watery tureen" of the toilet bowl the kind of loving attention that Keats bestowed on his Grecian urn. In place of "Beauty is truth", though, we are offered the rather less elevated insight that "Shit's a glimpse of Truth".

Patrick Kavanagh (who, incidentally, admired Ginsberg for his lack of "ponderosity") might have spoken for Adrienne Rich when he wrote, "Surely my God is feminine"; her truths are cast in a resolutely female light. While she has written no single poem of the calibre of Ginsberg's 'Kaddish' – a desolate portrait of a disturbed mother – several of the outstanding post-war collections have had Rich's name attached to them. Her work is more literary, less populist, than Ginsberg's; in the realm of politics, however, she too can overindulge the expectations of her audience. Poetry and politics co-exist in a delicate symbiosis; it takes only a minute chemical imbalance in the ratio of ideology to imagination for the wellsprings to become tainted and the poem to be rendered unfit for general consumption.

What has saved Rich's surest work from succumbing to the temptations of triumphalism and the rhetoric of the quarrel with others is her finely-tuned ear; her sensuous, yearning music transcends ephemeral argument and the divisive limitations of language itself. It is a classic case of the poem knowing more than the poet. She has written tellingly in her essay, 'Blood, Bread, and Poetry', that "any poet who mixes the poetry of the actual world with the poetry of sound interests and excites me more than I am able to say".

Adrienne Rich is not exactly a poet of hilarity and high jinks in the Ginsberg mode, nor does one sense that – like Ginsberg – she accepts that (for all the importance of ideological concerns) the poem as fibreglass pleasure craft is no less valid than the poem as steel-hulled container ship. There is a leaden quality about some of the freight in her latest collection, *Midnight Salvage*, an uncharacteristic lack of urgency in the writing that hinders the buoyancy of the poems:

> Had never expected hope would form itself
> completely in my time:: was never so sanguine
> as to believe old injuries could transmute easily
> through any singular event or idea :: never
> so feckless as to ignore the managed contagion
> of ignorance the contrived discontinuities...

Rich follows in the "footprints of light" of the photographer Tina Modotti and, more rewardingly, keeps "vigil" with the poet, René Char, during the French Resistance. Individual lines can be memorable ("art is a register of light"; "memory shooting its handheld frames") and the scene-setting is occasionally evocative – though the promise of the atmospheric openings is not fulfilled in the later sections of poems like 'Midnight Salvage' and '"The Night Has a Thousand Eyes"'. What quickens certain poems into life is memory – the memory of the childhood game "getting wilder as the lights come on" in 'A Long Conversation' (an over-long and over-loose mosaic of testimonies and quotations ranging across considerations of love, economics, language, torture, art, "struggles for justice" and much else) or the memory of a date with a "paraplegic GI" in 'Seven Skins', a vulnerable poem which is also a vivid snapshot of the Fifties:

Shall I drop you, he says, or shall
we go back to the room for a drink?

It's the usual question
a man has to ask it
a woman has to answer
you don't even think.

Rich still laudably insists on the subversive potential of language ("That the books are for personal use / only – could I swear it? / That not a word of them / is contraband – how could I prove it?"). But in affluent, unfazed America, assimilation continually neutralises subversion. Both the countercultural Ginsberg and the radical feminist Rich acquired lucrative university professorships, are published by prestigious mainstream houses, have been showered with adulation and honours (twelve lines worth of major prizes are listed on the dust jacket of Rich's gold-embossed hardback). Allen Ginsberg's work is done; he has become his admirers. Adrienne Rich still has work to do; resisting the expectations of her admirers will be an important part of it.

You can order these books POST-FREE from the PBS. See p.94 for details.

Hyphenate

by Kwame Dawes

LANGSTON HUGHES
Selected Poems
Serpent's Tail, £7.99
ISBN 1 85242 127 4

LANGSTON HUGHES WAS never uncomfortable in his own skin. In fact the business of writing about his skin was always important to him. Here was a poet who, granted lesser talent, could have easily been relegated to the dump pile of "race writers" whose credibility rested solely on the currency of their political ideologies and the manner in which they made the lyric a slave to the immediate tyranny of political commitment. There are many noble poets in that pile, incidentally, and the pile is a rubbish heap only because of the aesthetic values of the person doing the sweeping. But Hughes escaped such a fate eventually. Of course, there was a time, during the height of his career, when Hughes was not seen as a legitimate icon of America verse.

Not so today. In 1959, Hughes published his *Selected Poems*. This eclectic and wide-ranging collection of Hughes' work would establish him as a master poet in American letters. What is remarkable about Hughes is that he set the tone for black writers with the kinds of statements that still get people like Toni Morrison in trouble, but that, nonetheless, establish quite clearly that these writers understood themselves to be working within a distinctive aesthetic framework that had to be taken seriously and understood if their work was to be understood. While Hughes would not say, like Morrison has, that he writes primarily for a black audience, what he did say was that he was a black writer and that he wanted to be understood and read as a black writer. In his direct and defining essay, 'The Negro and the Racial Mountain', he establishes a credo that suggests that the only possible alternative to the instinct to declare oneself a black writer (if one is black) is to seek after that deeply questionable mantle of "just being a writer." The extent to which we understand that Hughes' declaration in his essay is radical and for some troubling can be seen in Tim O'Brien's attempt to equate his struggle with the idea of being a "Vietnam [war] writer" with Toni Morrison being a "black" writer. When asked if he could imagine what life and his work would be like if there was no Vietnam war he says:

> Not really, it's like asking Toni Morrison what life would've been like if she weren't black. You know, life gives us stuff: It gave Conrad the ocean, which he used in his stories. Life gave Updike domesticity and divorce and the suburbs, which he uses as material. And life gave me the Vietnam card. Yet I don't consider myself a Vietnam writer, any more than Morrison considers herself a black writer. We're writer writers. And we use what life gives us.

There is a false logic in that equation largely because it fails to recognize that the declaration of one's allegiances, affinities and labels brings with it a complex range of implications. For Morrison to declare herself a black writer has far different implications than for O'Brien to announce himself a Vietnam writer. More telling, however, is O'Brien's presumption that the "writer writers" status somehow transcends the status of the "hyphenated" writer. The assumption is that all writers prefer to be writers first and then whatever kind of writer next. For Hughes this was a false construct. He suggests that the black poet who declares that he does not want to be known as a black poet, but simply as a poet, is merely trying to be white and has bought into a series of stereotypes and expectations that surround being a black writer. Hughes argues, further, that there are very basic demands that will be made on the black poet who simply wants to be a poet, challenges that ultimately force him to accept white models and values. The non-hyphenated "poet", Hughes is arguing, is the white poet. The "universal" poet is the white European poet. That is the world in which we live. And the fall out from this desire to be just a poet for the black writer, is the necessary denial of the aesthetic values that emerge from black experience and black culture. For Hughes, this was not acceptable. And he determined to challenge such notions not by concealing his blackness, but by arguing that an aesthetic rooted in black experience is as complex, and artistically compelling as work done from a Euro-centric perspective. He planned to do a "jazz" in poetry: to assert the sheer brilliance of such black expression by introducing new paradigms of beauty.

What Hughes did was present America with a complex series of forms that emerged out of a cultural tradition that he respected and one that gave him meaning. Quite simply, were Hughes to have done what he was immensely capable of doing, that is become a conventional American lyric poet of the modernist ilk, the very significant impact of the blues on American literary culture would have been delayed for years or simply expunged.

Hughes' *Selected Poems* should reveal a few things to us. The first is that Hughes's relationship with the blues can be fairly equated with the relationship that a pioneering and gifted contemporary poet would have with Hip-Hop Music today. The challenges that such a poet would encounter are not different from those faced by Hughes. Hughes persisted and in the process introduced a quintessential American lyric form to American letters. The blues poem and the jazz poems evolved in Hughes because of a choice that he made. He chose to write poetry that was rooted in an African American aesthetic because he believed that such an aesthetic had profound relevance to American letters. Hughes' collection also reminds us of the dignity and authority that comes from a poet who has something to say about the society in which he lives. Many of the poems are political, deeply engaged and quite daring in the way they challenge the racism and injustice in American society. The effect is poetry that ranges from the lyrical splendor of 'A House in Taos':

> That there should be a barren garden
> About this house in Taos
> Is not so strange,
> Bu that there should be three barren hearts
> In this one house in Taos –
> Who carries ugly things to show the sun?

to the rhetorical incendiary, 'Harlem':

> Maybe it just sags
> like a heavy load
> Or does it explode?

Hughes' facility with sound and the gracefulness of simple language is wonderfully demonstrated in this collection. There are over two hundred poems collected here, all of them cast in the typically accessible simplicity of a Hughes' line, and yet many of them quite complex in their management of sentiment and experience. There are remarkable gems that come at you with fresh force each time you return to them. Here is his poem for Billie Holiday ('Song for Billie Holiday'). Observe the formal care – the use of the blues repetition in a way that does not draw attention to itself – the sweet variation on a single note:

> What can purge my heart
>   Of the song
>   And the sadness?
> What can purge my heart
>   But the song
>   Of the sadness?
> What can purge my heart
>   Of the sadness
>   Of the song?
> Do not speak of sorrow
>   With dust in her hair,
>   Or bits of dust in her eyes
> A chance wind blows there
>   The sorrow that I speak of
>   Is dusted with despair.

My one complaint about this Serpent's Tail edition is that there is little assistance given to the reader who is desperate to find a single poem by the first line or by title. There is no index of first lines or alphabetical listing of titles in the edition. I do understand the anxiety of transforming the book into an academic tome, but that is hardly likely with such a collection. Very little editorial work has been done here – this is a replication of the Hughes' selection of forty or so years ago, and while that has its own appeal, I think the contemporary reader would benefit from a better sense of the chronology of many of these poems.

Fine verse often lies in the distilled simplicity that ultimately demands our attention. Quite often the strength of a poet lies in the mastery of form so that the twisted and complex subjects of our sordid lives can be rendered with such delicacy that they become the stuff of archetype – not stripped of depth, but made into something lasting. Not all poets achieve this quality. Most of us putter around in the mire of our "complexity", so close to the strangeness of life that we fail to transcend it with the song of verse. If nothing else, the Blues is song regardless of what the Blues song is about. Hughes reminds us of this again and again in this collection of verse.

You can order this book POST-FREE from the PBS at £7.99. See p.94 for details.

JOHN GALLAS
RUDI

> Unlikely as a spook, she looked me up
> one flat weekend when, sick with hours ill-spent,
> I sought the buried spring of discontent.
> "Would you be happy up a mountain?" "Yup".
> "Mit crrrampons?" "Yup." "Und goggles?" "Yup." She smiled.
> I turned the tv off. "And so would I".
> It seemed unhelpful not to ask her why.
> "Because", she trilled, "you are the pregnant child
> of forty lives of sinews, boots and sky,
> whose strident habits thickened into fact
> and joined our genes". I sighed. The xerox act
> must catch some coloured fluff. She blurred. "Goodbye".
> I stayed inside. I dreamed my soul got free
> and lost its ache. I'm glad it isn't me.

TWO POEMS BY SHEENAGH PUGH
LOVE IS

Each time you go out, I wonder
if you'll meet them, the ones
warped beyond help,

bored enough to break
what can be broken:
benches, saplings, bones.

Love is knowing they're out there
even when they aren't.

I see their smiles
as they call you. I see
your face, open,

trusting, as they take you
to some unwatched place.
I see your eyes

widen as they turn
on you, and I think
they laugh, then,

at your pain, but still more
at your surprise; how easy
it was to fool you.

Love is dreaming things they could do
that even they don't guess.

Up to the moment
when you walk through the door
whole, smiling, safe,

you are lying in the dark
I made in my head,
and their grins are fixed

where my blade etched them.
Your name, which they never
cared to ask,

I burn carefully,
with a flourish of pokerwork,
into their flesh.

Love is knowing I could do
anything they could.

GOING TO LIVERPOOL

I am a middle-aged woman
travelling on business
and I'm going to Liverpool,

where I'll take time out
to visit Albert Dock
and the museum

where my youth is preserved.
The fashions I followed,
the songs I knew by heart,

the faces that convulsed
my own into screams
and sobs, they'll all be there.

I'm going to Liverpool,
and it is autumn.
The fields outside Leominster

lie in stubble; the leaves
of Ludlow's trees are jaundiced
and flushed with the fever

that says they're finished.
The ticket collector
said *Thank you, Madam.*

My daughter's grown up
and my mother's dead,
and between the pages

of the notebook
where I'm writing this
I keep a yellowed ticket

to a match, a picture
of an actor, Edwin Morgan's reply
to my fan letter,

and I'm going to Liverpool
because I'm the kind
that always will.

ANTHONY HOWELL
BRIDGE

I think I see what you see in the rock:
A rabbit's leaping shadow, then an ox.
They thought they saw what we see in the cleft
Above the gap a stream shares with a draught:
The dewlap, then the muzzle to the left,
The jawbone touched by light above that plant.
We think we see what they saw
– Or what they thought they saw –
The nostrils of a horse, lionesses' eyes, lionesses
Everywhere around their cavern and the bears'
Eyes in each dent; the flanks of a bison
In this fold, that crack. Nothing
Magic about it, apart from what
They saw or thought they saw above an arch
Hewn in the rock by an ox-bow stream;
Lying here all wet, like us perhaps,
But looking out for lionesses, lionesses.

JOHN GREENING
JULY 12TH
after hearing Evelyn Glennie

Protestantism beats the air polyrhythmical,
crowds press to the barriers at Drumcree.

While here in a middle England chapel, we file
to occupy all sides of a loaded stage.

Bombs home-made from treaties soaked in hatred
burn the Garvaghy Road. We look at an oil-drum

or turn a discreet page. The R.U.C. get out
their riot shields, the troops load rubber bullets.

We prepare our applause, a tam-tam waiting
to swell, a secular gamelan. Black hats

attend to the Grand Master of the Orange Order.
We – to a loose gown and hair, bare feet.

Peace is forgotten, all palms are closed to it.
But she picks up two sticks and begins a new

piece called *Darkness to Light*, frightening a child
in the front row, who has to be carried out,

but exploding into the dance-floor colours of this
converted nave a wave to thrill those of us

perched nervously on the edge. In Ulster
this night three children are set on fire

in a sectarian arson attack. Darkness to
light, the marimba reminds us, glowing its

optimism against the death rattle and attack of
drumkit, Drumcree and deafening Lambeg drums.

Waxing and Waning

by Rod Mengham

JOHN ASHBERY

Girls on the Run
Carcanet, £6.95
ISBN 1 85754 435 8

THE COVER ILLUSTRATION to the Carcanet edition of John Ashbery's new book features part of a Henry Darger painting entitled 'Storm Brewing'. It shows a sky filling up with black ink over a landscape of busy flower arrangements, while at the centre is a group of pubescent girls running from right to left and from middle ground to foreground. This scenario shares all the most important contours of Ashbery's poem, the twenty one chapters of which use the paintings of Darger as a pretext for their own mixture of brooding elemental disorder, indulgence of juvenile cameraderie and a terror of the fate of all cartoon characters who fail to outrun the inevitable. Ashbery's version of the inevitable often starts as the weather only to turn, by giddying degrees, into various things much more potent and menacing.

What is most disturbing about these shifts and mutations is the rapidity with which single events are linked to extremely long perspectives: "The tainted fir-trees / fell over and were loam". This movement goes in both directions, panning in and out of the present, speeding up a whole range of slow natural processes into an immediacy that devolves onto a sense of "permanency / sliding toward day". In a whole variety of ways, the writing plays constantly with the idea of losing its footing, despite always recovering its poise and nimbleness for limited periods.

There is a recurrent fascination with thin membranes, fragile thresholds between states of security and of insecurity, between conditions that are under control and those that aren't. One of the most significant phrases in the book is "the other side", usually accompanying either a curiosity or an anxiety about what lies on the other side of any given experience. Negotiating the threshold between the known and unknown involves both the imagining of the other side and the discovery that what is known because it is familiar can be profoundly baffling, paradoxically "the indecipherable, / the knowable past".

A lack of nerve over the testing of these boundaries that prove so deceptive is domesticated by constant expressions of an unwillingness to leave the house, or even single rooms, and a preference for planning schedules for one day at a time. Just as the timetables prove impossible to maintain, the spatial co-ordinates are equally prone to sabotage. Local containment strategies are overtaken by hints of obscure universal disasters: numerous floods, climate changes, lava flows and cataclysmic explosions – various kinds of "big ones". The Darger paintings maintain a facade of charming consternation but seem deeply phobic in origin. Ashbery's gallivanting teams of characters likewise get sucked into other and more sinister dimensions. Their stories follow the pattern associated with the Pied Piper, seduction followed by abduction and irrevocable loss: "Come, it's silver, children, the unbearable letdown / has gone under the hill to bide its time. Centuries shall pass away this way".

To a quite surprising extent, the more cryptic vocabularies of the poem revolve around questions of salvation. There is a high incidence of expressions of a desire to escape, be delivered, be saved. The frequent narrative divagations almost always lead back to the conceptual structures of narratives of faith and vocation, and here the model is *Pilgrim's Progress*. The particular girls on the run in these pages, leaving rooms and houses that they feel thay shouldn't, tend to go by names such as Tidbit, Dimples, Persnickety Peggy; but another cohort of characters requires the names of Hopeful, Pliable, Talkative. Diction and phrasing is regularly Bunyanesque: "so they set to work, with a right good will"; "and he betook himself on his two legs"; "so that everything was as it had been before"; "seven times seven ages later".

The fixation that underlies Bunyan's narrative of delays and obstructions is the other side of inevitability. It makes running away from a cloudburst lead ultimately to apocalypse and a sense of election. Although misgivings about destiny and destination remain right up to the last chapter: "So we faced the new day, / like a pilgrim who sees the end of his journey deferred forever".

I know this sounds ridiculously top-heavy in a characteristically sly Ashbery poem, but the tonal shifts in his work have always been able to travel immense distances even in a single line, as they do here in a much more than whimsical conflation of abandonment, revocation, agoraphobia: "I'll write you from that solemn coast, / but you must promise never to remember me, never speak of me, / until we are found at last behind the bathroom door, with the broom". It is typical of Ashbery that that final-comic absurdity can accommodate, but not defuse, both trauma and obsession; especially typical of this poem and its shuddering complexity of tones that "secretly... waxes as it wanes".

You can order this book POST-FREE from the PBS at £6.95. See p.94 for details.

Out of this World

by Ian McMillan

JOHN KINSELLA

Visitants

Bloodaxe, £ 7.95
ISBN 1 85224 505 0

A JOKEY PRESS release with *Visitants* suggests that John Kinsella has been made Poet in Residence in outer space, because a number of the poems in the book refer to extra-terrestrial visitors, but I'd like to suggest that Kinsella should be made (and this is a big Poetry Place) Poet in Residence in The World, which is a much warmer place than that vast emptiness beyond the clouds.

Anyone who has read Kinsella's fat *Poems 1980-1994* (also published by Bloodaxe) will know that The World is a great place for Kinsella; he revels in Big Things, Big Concepts, Big Spaces. Visitants begins with 'A Bright Cigar-Shaped Object Hovers Over Mount Pleasant' where a clawed hand reaches out from the object "to drag me in, the cigar / -shaped object stopped stock still /and hovering like the sun..." and ends with 'Ascension', where "believers" "waiting for the next time, / waiting for a new Director to lead them into the sun, / to full knowledge, immortality; oneness" and in between he visits the wilder shores of Robotics, Phenomenology, Divining, the Theory of Forms and Alienation. Unlike some poets who flash their learning at you like mirrors designed to dazzle in the sun, Kinsella just tell you stuff because he's excited, and you grow to love him for it.

It's hard to quote from poems (and this isn't a copout: you know how much I like quoting) because quoting from them would be like that moment when you're eating a bacon sandwich in public and you try to bite a little bit of the bacon off delicately and the whole slice flops out from between the bread and hangs from your mouth like the tongue of a shoe. That's how it is with these poems. Quote the lines from 'Visitant Eclogue' "Well I said to the missis that something pretty odd / was happening out here, this being the third night / lights have appeared over the Needlings; and she / said stay clear Ben Rollins, stay clear, don't go..." and there seems to be no place to stop, and soon the whole slice of bacon is hanging over your chin and you've quoted the entire thing, a sequence owing a little to Edwin Morgan where the thoughts and words of the farmer we've already heard from are juxtaposed with the utterings of the visitant "radiant inner heart countertracking epicycloidal / windrows and approaching harvest, as if to probe your body / like a contagion that'll never let you go...". You could say that Kinsella's work is hard to cut into chunks because the lines often run on and there are rarely handy little stanza-nets to catch your quotes in, and that's partly it, but part of the quotability problem is because it's the very overwhelmingness, the rushes of enthusiasm, the sense of a rollercoaster-ride that you get with the best music or the best conversation that makes these poeuns work.

I won't quote, then; I'll just recommend moods, styles, visions. The book is divided into four sections, each self-contained, each contributing to the larger *Visitants* whole. The first section, 'Making Contact', concentrates on a lost childood where the visitants appear for the first time and take their place in an odd (to me, anyway, not perhaps to Kinsella) Australian landscape where the children squeeze their eyes tight shut to make colours come, make pinhole cameras and see strange objects rising out of the sand. Kinsella's skill is to evoke childlike wonder but to leave us wondering which is memory and which is invention, which is screwing your eyes tight and which is looking through a peephole camera. The second section, 'A Theory of Forms', is full of experiment and references to other arts, from 'High Noon – A Visitation' a poem after a painting by Edward

REVIEWS

Hopper, to 'Dispossession', an angry list about the appropriation of Native Australian art. Section three, 'Body Snatching', returns overtly to the Visitants theme, and looks at the impact of visitants, whether they're aliens on Earth or Pat Rafter on Bermuda. It's clear from this section, and from the whole book and from the whole of Kinsella's work, that he's against colonisation and imperialism, whether actual or artistic. Section four, particularly with the long piece 'nature morte: Oh Rhetoric!' seems to question the very possibility of writing being able to do anything useful, something which Kinsella seems to answer by the huge waterfall of his work.

It amazes me that Kinsella, despite his huge output, isn't better known; maybe I should have quoted more to try and get people to buy the book. On the other hand, there's no point nibbling at the bacon: you've got to get the whole lot in your mouth at once. Enjoy!

You can order this book POST-FREE from the PBS at £7.95. See p.94 for details.

Pride of Place in Irish Poetry

by Conor Kelly

PETER FALLON

News of the World
Gallery Press, £7.95
ISBN 1 85235 214 0

BERNARD O'DONOGHUE

Here Nor There
Chatto & Windus, £8.99
ISBN 0 7011 6800 5

CONOR O'CALLAGHAN

Seatown
Gallery Press, £6.95
ISBN 1 85235 242 6

VONA GROARKE

Other People's Houses
Gallery Press, £6.95
ISBN 1 85235 240 X

GERARD FANNING

Working for the Government
Dedalus, £5.95
ISBN 1 901233 38 3

BRENDAN KENNELLY

The Singing Tree
Abbey Press, £8.00
ISBN 1 901617 09 2

The Man Made of Rain
Bloodaxe, £7.95
ISBN 1 85224 455 0

BRENDAN CLEARY

Sacrilege
Bloodaxe, £7.95.
ISBN 1 85224 460 7

FROM YEATS'S SLIGO to Heaney's Mossbawn and Glanmore, from Kavanagh's Monaghan to Muldoon's Moy, from Kinsella's Dublin to Carson's maps of Belfast, a sense of place has always been a significant feature of Irish poetry. Furthermore, that sense of place is often accompanied by a sense of pride. In one way or another these eight books under review offer intriguing and differing responses to the hold the landscape of Ireland continues to have on the poets who live there.

Peter Fallon
Although Peter Fallon is a major publisher of poetry in Ireland, he has set his press and his presence, not in a metropolitan centre, but in a farm in the heart of the Irish countryside. "All I ever wanted", he claims in one poem, "was / to make a safe house in the midlands". In *News of the World*, a selection from his earlier work, along with some new poems, he explores the life, the lore, the landscape of his chosen fields. He also attempts to find

a language – quiet, intent and inquisitive – adequate to the farming population among whom he lives. This is a difficult enterprise and at times the syntax slips too comfortably into a brogue that is fluent, lucid, colloquial, but not entirely convincing, like a Meryl Streep accent. The poems are at their worst, their most moist and mushy, when dealing with historical matters; they are at their best when dealing, in a laconic manner, with local matters, local characters, local lore. To call Peter Fallon a laureate of lambing, a chronicler of sheep-farming, is, in fact, to praise the fidelity, the respect and the resonance he brings to bear on his own pride of place: "My part in this is reverence".

Another, distant place occupies a second sequence of poems, 'The Deerfield Series: Strength of Heart'. Deerfield, in Western Massachusetts, was the frontier outpost of the English settlement of New England and the site of celebrated historical events, commemorated in some of the poems. "I have tried in the poem's various parts", a note tells us, "to enter history, geography and mythology to comprehend a place and its fate." The poems constantly try but, missing the sense of community so evident in the Irish poems, they remain trying and tendentious. There is history but no historical resonance; geography but no sense of place; mythology, but no animating myth. The conclusion, when it arrives is too bland, too banal and too basic: "Be worthy of this life. And, Love the world".

A third, concluding sequence, 'The Heart's Home', is more successful in its sense of place. A poem like 'The Bandon Road: Sight of It' twists and turns, like the road it describes, in a loving evocation of the adventitious, a skill Fallon has honed to his adept measurements as his syntax sways through an "array of wonder." And when, in another poem, he goes out "to check a lazy ewe / in labour", the poet is in familiar territory and the power to render the natural world in realistic and resonant detail becomes a pleasure, one of many in this book.

Bernard O'Donoghue

The first poem in Bernard O'Donoghue's latest book has a mythical narrator who is "homesick / For Ireland" but, unwelcome there and forbidden to land, is

> Fated
> To sail for ever in the middle seas, outcast
> Alike from the one shore and the other.

Appropriately entitled *Here Nor There*, this intriguing and inventive collection is taut with the tensions of exclusion, particularly from the poet's rural West Cork background. While Peter Fallon attempts to integrate himself into his environment, O'Donoghue acknowledges, at every turn, his own sad sense of distance from the heart of the localities he celebrates with tenderness and a wry sense of territorial possession. Yet that possessiveness, lovingly dwelt on, is of someone who has lost his possessions. And so, as the childhood memories of his Irish upbringing animate these poems, a counter current is evident, one in which education, exile and a mythological sense of the world offer an ironic perspective on the author more than the author's world. At times it is like adding ice cubes to Irish whiskey – an acquired (often abroad) taste.

The poems are at their best when dealing, not with pride of place, but with the people who brought those places to life. Occasionally the reminiscences become sentimental, coated in a sepia haze; but, at their sharpest, they are touched by what one poem cleverly calls "the architecture of the spirit". And that spirit, elegiac and ironic, is also generous. Name after Irish name is invoked, as the past is evoked and the pressure of person and place explored. Astutely aware of how pride and "a lifetime of / Taking real things for shades" can inflict pain, the book ends with a wonderful account – 'Ter Conatus' – of a sibling relationship strained from being neither here nor there, neither together nor alone; in effect, a story, an elegy and, that rare object, a beautifully achieved poem.

Conor O'Callaghan

The title of Conor O'Callaghan's much acclaimed second collection, *Seatown*, is also the title of two or, in its Irish form, three poems all dealing with his home in the coastal border town of Dundalk. In these poems, and in many others, he reveals a remarkable eye and ear for the petty matter-of-fact details of contemporary Irish life. Rejecting "the Atlantic guff" of much Irish poetry, he turns his poetic attention to a bleaker "sanctuary of sorts", one in which realistic detail achieves artistic distinction: "But give me a dreary eastern town that isn't vaguely romantic". While he cannot always keep a romantic Irish lyricism at bay, and acknowledges as much – "me // a token romantic" – he does manage to create a hard-edged, Beckett-like bleakness which is skilfully made to fit the geographical circumstances described. Although the blurb, talking about Dundalk, sees the poetry as "an unqualified hymn to its rundown charm", there is plenty that is qualified, little that is charming and even less that could be called hymn-like. But there is humour in adversity and that humour is sardonic, even sour. 'The Oral Tradition' may be just a dirty joke; but an astute sense of place gives it a poetic frisson and a clever use of language gives it a poetic wit. And that clever use of the demotic and the descriptive goes some way to relieving the bleakness of a book in which the most common word is probably "no".

Another way of relieving the bleakness is to acknowledge other, more feminine intuitions. In 'She Waits for News...' the poet may choose not to understand the emotions he so eloquently describes, but the ability to admit into the ambit of his ambition a counter current is an invigorating strength. And when, in the concluding poem, 'Slip', about a road from the town to the sea, he states

> There is no time
> to dwell on metaphors
> for an aimless life...

it may seem like another, more final rejection of the redemptive, romantic power of poetry. But, whether or not the poems in this intriguing collection achieve the status of metaphor, this book and this poetry is far from aimless.

Vona Groarke

Vona Groarke also lives in Dundalk. (Internal evidence in both books suggest these two poets are married to each other.) But her sense of place is one that dwells on interiors, on estates, houses, rooms, furniture. Of the thirty three poems in her second collection, *Other People's Houses*, twenty seven of them have the word "house" or "home" in their titles. Although some could be called light verse, the very lightness of touch has the charm and neatness of a well kept housing estate. 'Open House', for example, describes, in neat couplets, a neat estate where "at first glance every house looks much the same". But the poem, like the estate, deserves a second, even a third glance, one in which ironic wit and a civilised curiosity combine to produce a poem where "something more than just mortar and bricks" is being investigated, even interrogated. It ends in two separate bedrooms divided only by a brick wall where ideas of distance and desire are playfully exchanged. And that play, of rhythm, rhyme, stanza, sonnet, song, is everywhere evident in this amusing, even amazing, sequence. 'House Wine', for example, is admitted to the sequence via the pun in the title, but it exudes an enticing bouquet.

Not all the poems indulge in the light touch. The sequence becomes more sombre as it looks at other, odder houses: lighthouses being made, like their inhabitants, redundant; workhouses where a history of poverty pervades the surroundings; slaughterhouses where the fate of animals chills the poet "to the bone"; and an empty courthouse where, that pervasive wit again, "silence is upheld" and "the windows, in their cases, rattle on". And there is a humanity in housing and in houses lost, left or abandoned which the best of these poems expresses with subtlety, depth and an emotional resonance that is as unusual as it is welcome. As the sequence comes to an end, it becomes more personal, a reaching out beyond bricks and mortar to what remains beyond "other people's houses". There is a pride in more than place here, a pride in poetry that makes this book a welcome house in the estate of Irish poetry.

Gerard Fanning

Further down the east coast of Ireland is the seaside resort of Bettystown, a popular holiday retreat for Dubliners in the fifties and sixties. Here, where the clay is "like ground tarragon, / With its stench of burnished brine", Gerard Fanning sets the opening sequence of his second collection *Working for the Government*. The poems subtly navigate the terrain not only in geographical and historical terms, but also in psychological terms. These poems take that stable cliché of Irish poetry – the father-son relationship – and reinvigorate it with a plangent air of nostalgia and, ultimately, grief. The sense of place is palpable, not only in this sequence of seven poems, but also in the rest of this lithe and lyrical collection. While some of the poems are set in Italian or American cities, the best of them are in Irish locations where the poet, working for the government as a civil servant or taking a welcome holiday break from that work, explores, in musical terms, routes that vanish into silence. For it is in their music – their subtle rhythms, haunting rhymes, eloquent syntax – that these poems achieve their finest expression. And it is in the silence surrounding them that they achieve an aura that is hard to define but easy to enjoy.

Where music meets silence, where land meets

sea, where darkness meets light, where a sense of place meets an intimation of emptiness, that is where these poems inhabit, exuding meaning as a ship "breathes its drift of sooty snow". In one of the best poems, 'Dusk Walks', a central message is suggested

> The noise of the world is so terrible
> We can endure it only
> By being coated with drowse.

To be coated in drowse is not to be drowsy. It is, rather, a recognition of the manner in which music, particularly the music of poetry, can sustain itself against the terrible noises that surround and sometimes attack it. This is another welcome collection.

Brendan Kennelly

My welcome for Brendan Kennelly is far more subdued. Subtlety, drowse, sinuous syntax and suggestive ambiguities are not the provenance of his poetry. His music is louder, more strident and far more self-assertive. Among the most prolific of Irish poets, he has, typically, two books under review, both accompanied by an "author's note", both in free-floating, full throated forms, both self-mocking and self-centred.

The Singing Tree is the slighter and slimmer of the two, "a bridge poem, an otherstructure based on disruption and transference." The transference involves war, violence, murder, suicide, money, illness and poverty. The transference involves the poet – "I am insatiable energy" – giving a voice to objects: a wall, a bullet, the tide, skin, a scar, a worm, a raindrop, a key, a freckle and a park bench. Imaginative? Yes. Accomplished? No. All the voices sound the same. Everything Kennelly touches turns to Kennelly. Although the poems try "to step out of the cage of self into something else", the bridges are not well made. Or, to put it another way, this singing tree has no roots.

A second, more substantial collection, *The Man Made of Rain*, is also more ambitious. Written after major heart surgery, it is a vision poem. As the author's note puts it: "I saw a man made of rain... He spoke to me and took me on journeys... He led me to different places". The poems, then, are a record of those journeys, a rhapsodic report on the different places encountered in transit. And therein lies the problem. The sense of place is too inchoate, too marginal, to register. Although the book is populated by people, some drawn from memory like the poet's father, some drawn from street graffiti, they all exist in a geographical vacuum. There are numerous references to the poet's home in Dublin and his roots in Kerry, but they are all swept up in the visionary whirlwind. It is easy to admire the liveliness, the courage, the defiance in the face of death and the epic intensity of a vision doggedly pursued. It is harder to admire the actual poems.

Brendan Kennelly has now become Ireland's Walt Whitman: energetic, expansive, exuberant, prolific and excessive. America certainly needed such a figure towards the end of the last century. Whether or not, at the end of this century, Ireland needs such a poet is a debatable question. Kennelly enters that debate with characteristic brio. Like him or not, you certainly cannot ignore him.

Brendan Cleary

A commendation on the blurb of Brendan Cleary's latest collection, *Sacrilege*, refers to him as "the eternal teenager of Irish poetry", an appropriate comment on a poet whose sense of place has the aura of a student's armpit. The poems are set in bed-sit land, in a world of wild drink and drug parties where the characters end up "crashing on the floor / looking for lost bits of Moroccan hashish", having staggered drunkenly through urban landscapes in search of more drink, quick sex and lashings of "simple philosophy". Although Tyneside is mentioned, the setting is insubstantial enough to be anywhere the louche life can be lived in earnest. This is laddish poetry – "After a feed of pints & a late-night smoking session" – albeit with a rhythmic hangover. Read quickly, the book has an immediacy that is, at times, galvanising. These poems are not just culled from literary magazines, but from a radio breakfast show. Some also belong to that genre known as performance poetry. But what stands up on stage can go limp on the page, particularly if read when sober. The manic moaning of this "sad dysfunctional poet" becomes repetitive, tiresome and adolescent. At times it is like reading Peter Reading in short pants. And when it comes to the final sequence, 'The New Rock 'n' Roll', its celebration of rock legends is just too embarrassing to be digested. Give me Paul Muldoon's record collection any day. Or maybe I am just too old for all this.

You can order these books POST-FREE from the PBS. See p.94 for details.

Lyrical Gangstas

By Robert Potts

**The Message:
Crossing the tracks
between poetry and pop**
Edited by Roddy Lumsden
and Stephen Troussé,
The Poetry Society, £4.95
ISBN 1 9007 7118 7

Oral
Edited by Sarah-Jane Lovett
Hodder, £6.99
ISBN 0 340750510

NEATLY COINCIDING WITH National Poetry Day's search for The Nation's Favourite Song Lyric (won by John Lennon with 'Imagine'), Roddy Lumsden's *The Message* is the product of his work under the Poetry Places scheme, which has seen many British poets working in or around zoos, supermarkets, law firms, museums and the like. Lumsden has been given the elbow room, in a small but attractive book, to explore the relationship between pop lyrics and poetry. A deliberate "gallimaufry" of poems, articles, lists and discussions, it sensibly attempts neither binding definitions (of either poetry or song lyrics) nor evaluations (of the Keats v. Dylan type). Instead it moves, with patient enthusiasm, through the differences and similarities between the two forms and, more humorously, between the lifestyles of poets and musicians.

It is, necessarily, impressionistic; it is also, winningly, passionate and funny. Lumsden, as a practising poet, and the writer of subtle but accessible verses, appreciates the richness and complexity that poetry can be capable of (indeed, one of his most laudable war-cries in this book is that a volume of poetry selling at seven or eight quid needs to contain poems that demand to be read more than once); but he also loves the potency and aptness of the better song lyrics, which hit home (and are remembered) more often than poetry. For anyone of a certain age or younger, their past (and particularly their adolescence) will have been soundtracked by what they were listening to at the time; and hearing those songs again will recall such memories. It is not uncommon for people who claim to have a poor memory for poetry to remember every line of a song when they hear it, even after many years have passed.

Lumsden is frank about how limp even the best songs can seem when torn from the moods and rhythms of their music and their delivery, though I would maintain that this is not always true. *Oral*, an anthology of "poems, sonnets, lyrics and the like" seems set to prove his point, though. Sarah-Jane Lovett, in her introduction, writes, with the ahistorical zeal of the young, that "we have seen a huge resurgence of interest in and redisovery of the spoken word and its potential... people everywhere are talking, shouting, reciting, rapping, blurting, singing, and this surely enriches our lives". It is an interesting view; that expression in itself is enriching, rather than what is expressed. It does sometimes seem as if everybody is, indeed, making more noise, but one does wonder if all of it is worth listening to, or even whether anyone is listening at all.

Oral does contain a few good pieces, mainly by poets who have opted for a traditional, ballad-like form and a simple lyric (like Alan Jenkins) or stick to verse rather than pop poetry (like Roddy Lumsden himself), or lyricists (like Jarvis Cocker or Nick Cave) who do know the value of form and stylised expression. It is also gently amusing that the alphabeticization of contributors has Hugo Wiliams rubbing shoulders with Robbie Williams. But the bulk of the book is trite beyond belief; and if rhythm is going to be imparted solely by delivery, rather than formal construction, some of these pieces should be reserved for performance. Lovett admires "the telling it like it is" and its "honesty and lack of artifice", and insists that "what therefore must be acknowledged is its existence". Well, I hereby acknowledge the existence of artless self-expression. I wouldn't want to pay for it, though.

Lumsden, on the other hand, is sensible and ecumenical, noting the difference – in style, effect, audience reaction and so forth – between performance poetry and page-based poetry, and suggests that practitioners of both should share more gigs. He also, rightly, points out that some page-based poets are rivetting in performance. Having recently seen James Fenton electrify a large audience at the Cheltenham Literary Festival, and having fond memories of stand-up routines from Don Paterson and Simon Armitage, I'd happily agree with that too. Lumsden's offerings in *Oral* include 'My Pain' (apparently, and intriguingly, "from *Roddy*

Lumsden is Dead"), which I only mention because it cites some lines by the Irish singer Cathal Coughlan. Lumsden rightly praises Coughlan's work (with the bands Microdisney and the Fatima Mansions), and admits in *The Message* that he is "the only songwriter I have plundered for phrases for poems". Coughlan alternates between a bloodied personal lyricism and excoriating political satire (his 'Popemobile to Paraguay', for example, dealt with links between the Vatican and the CIA in right-wing South American countries, heavy stuff for a song lyric). It was a real delight to find that he has fans as intelligent as Lumsden.

There is praise, from Michael Bracewell and others, for artists like Morrissey, Bob Dylan and REM too, along with more recent groups who I am perhaps too old to have heard of. The nicest thing about *The Message* is that it takes both genres seriously, but not too seriously. As a lover of both, I have, at times, devoted as earnest attention to pop lyrics as, I have to, say, *The Lyrical Ballads*, and am exactly the sort of figure lampooned, in a "hidden" track on the first Mansun LP, 'Open Letter to the Lyrical Trainspotter':

> The lyrics aren't supposed to mean that much
> They're just a vehicle for a lovely voice
> They aren't supposed to mean that much.

You can order *The Message* direct from The Poetry Society. See the back cover advert for details.

SIÂN HUGHES
SOAP

The boy's face is his father's first stroke of luck –
before the child can lift his head from the blanket
wool manufacturers compete for the negatives.

It makes his Daddy's day to see him sit up and smile:
"Freddy, show your dimples to the nice gentleman,
I'm through at the elbows". Nothing pays like soap.

Ten foot high, dressed in bubbles, he spends the winter
riding the sides of trolley buses up to Princess Street.
It's enough to make his sisters get down and walk.

Blanco pays the doctor's bills, *Sudso* goes on drink,
Pears pays for one and one-in-arms to America,
where the boys can cut his teeth in style, on steak.

NEWS/COMMENT

STOP

Craig Raine is as omnipresent again as he was in the early '80s. His new magazine *Areté* was presaged by a gust of publicity blowing through the papers concerning his poem 'A la recherche du temps perdu' (do you think that title is trying to nudge us into something?). The poem is printed here in this first issue ("Issue One of *Areté* is dedicated to Valerie Eliot"). One of Raine's specialities is the close reading of other poets and critics with the aim of proving they're no good. Tim Kendall, Michael Hofmann and Helen Vendler get shown up here and Craig's assistant Jeremy Noel-Tod is wheeled on to prove that Les Murray isn't much good either. So let's turn the close-reading lens on Raine's own poem:

> At the station, you took of my specs
> And kissed me all over my face.
>
> I was your 'Wizzledy man'
> And you were pleased to see me again.
>
> We ate a quiche, a quiche Lorraine,
> Quiche hadn't reached England then.

The poem is a farrago of prissy affectation, erotomania, and crashing banality in pretty even proportions. Like all writers who over-reach themselves he can't see the looming pits of bathos:

> What else do I remember? ...
> your black smoking bush
> [at which point an image looms of the old joke "Do you smoke after intercourse?" "I don't know, I've never looked", which rather spoils the erotic reverie]
> the dark brown lips
> labyrinthine as a molten iris.
>
> The most beautiful I've ever seen.
> The most beautiful that's ever been.

Raine seems to feel that with his history of metaphoric excess he's earned the right to the plainness of the last couplet. The poem is littered with such banalities and ends: "This is my purpose. // To make you real. / To make you see, to make you feel, // to make you hear. // To make you here". Just before this we have:

> I borrowed your teeth for Judina
> And gave your cunt to Ivinskaya.
>
> Disjecta membra scattered everywhere.

That "disjecta membra" is perfect: the whole thing reeks of "play your cards right, darlin' and you'll end up in my *'oover*, I'm a genius, you know". But the machine broke down some time ago and merely scatters wispy fluff everywhere.

In the rest of the magazine there are some good things, mostly on European themes: Jerzy Jarniewicz on the quarrel between Czeslaw Milosz and Zbigniew Herbert, Raine's wife, Anne Pasternak Slater, on 'A Bergen-Belsen Correspondence', but the magazine is obviously going to be a magnet for pseuds. There's a page of minimalist nullity from Harold Pinter and Frederick Raphael mincing around on Flaubert. A letters page has Raine berating hapless courier services for not expediting his important packages. The whole is more the Crankiness of Craig than the *Criterion* reborn.

ASTERIX!!!***ETC

http://www.literarytranslation.com is the new website developed by the British Council and the Centre for Literary Translation at Norwich, highlighting the joys and pitfalls of translation. Translation is a inherently web-friendly idea and the site makes good use of the web's strengths. The section on *Asterix*, which is full of challenging puns in the French has captions which translate instantly on mouse rollover. There's also a page on the translations of *Trainspotting* swear words into Joual, the Quebecois French dialect, a Bible translation workshop and much general information.

PBS EXCLUSIVE BOOK SUPPLY SERVICE

From this issue on readers of *Poetry Review* can receive most of the books featured in the magazine post-free by mail order from the Poetry Book Society. If your local bookshop's idea of a poetry section is a shelf of Keats Collected and two tatty copies of *The Waste Land* this is the service you've been waiting for! Call 0208 8870 8403 between 9.30am and 5.30pm Mon-Fri to make your order, quoting *"Poetry Review"*. All major credit/debit cards accepted, including Switch.

ENDSTOPS

CORREX

Apologies to Paul Muldoon and Rod Mengham for losing the last line of Mengham's review of *Hay* (Vol 89 No 3, p84). The piece should end "Rehearsing those uses while simultaneously extemporizing new ones might not prevent the sky falling but we are reminded of its importance, and its importance is safeguarded, by the number of times this particular hay-maker hits his nails on the head".

NET VERSE

Subtitles can be revealing. That of Vispo at http://www.vispo.com/ is "Langu(im)age" so it will probably come as little surprise to learn that I've bookmarked it with the description "interesting and a bit weird". It has a lot of attractively produced dynamic poetry by Jim Andrews. Words change shape, morph into other words, roll around the screen in interesting and attractive ways. It also has a RealAudio section with intriguing renderings of Jim's poetry, and some from Martha Cinabar.

The subtitle of the Thimblepoets site at http://www.thimblepoets.org/ is "poetry that protects", which didn't inspire a lot of confidence. Indeed, the chatrooms and message boards of this site are best avoided. Its library area does have a useful collection of literary resources such as dictionaries and thesauruses. Another site worth visiting for its growing list of resource links is The Daisy Chain at http://www.suite101.com/myhome.cfm/The_Daisy_Chain

Some sites worth visiting for the poems themselves include John (*Jacket*) Tranter's homepage at http://www.alm.aust.com/~tranterj/index.html; The Works and Quirks of Michael Snider at http://msnider.home.mindspring.com/; and Larry Jaffe's expansive site at http://www.lgjaffe.com/

A new literary resource from Scotland is The Book Town Search Engine at http://www.scotlit.com/ which is a searchable guide to books and literature on the web. It's quick and straightforward to use, though it needs to expand its database, which is currently a bit patchy.

Cauldron and Net at http://www.StudioCleo.com/cauldron/ is a literary magazine that uses lots of multimedia. There's some good quality material, but the site plays tricks with your browser which you may or may not enjoy. You'll probably need to restart Netscape or Internet Explorer after a visit here, so make it the last point of call.

Send details of other places to stop off to me at peter@hphoward.demon.co.uk

LETTERS

TICKINGS OFF

Dear Peter,

I received my copy of the latest *Poetry Review* today. Normally, I think it's a big mistake to respond to criticisms of what one's written. However, I was surprised to find myself paraded as someone unable even to spell correctly – in a piece about the Geoffrey Dearmer Prize short list by Sheenagh Pugh (Vol 89 No 3, p.12) in which she rather too obviously relished the role of teacher addressing sub-standard pupils. As at this point she was discussing spelling, competence and respect for words, rather than her response to the poems, I should like to set things straight.

My own reaction on coming across a usage that I don't know is, not to reach for the red pencil but to have a look at the complete *OED*. There, Sheenagh Pugh would have found, as I did to my pleasure on first writing my poem of this title, that "aqueduct" is glossed with "also aquae-, aquaduct", indicating an alternative spelling certainly acceptable in previous centuries. In a poem about the feel and sense of water in a landscape, I was glad to have the possibility of a form which gave greater presence to the "aqua-" of the more usual English prefix and the "agua" and "acqua" of other European languages. Some performances of Schubert's *Trout Quintet* have a more "watery" feel to the playing than others; I hoped to get the most liquid feeling into my poem here.

True, friends did wonder if this would get across to all readers. I replied that a necessarily long footnote would be a rather pretentious encumbrance to explain one letter. Naively, as I now know, I argued also that, in writing "at this level" (as Pugh puts it), a different usage "three times in one poem" would surely suggest to most readers that some particular point was being made. Rather than the unreflecting conclusion that, really, other people are surprisingly incompetent!

One of the nice things about a formal code of language is that one can, given an alert listener, signal additional thoughts with even a slight variation on the standard message. In the job I've done over the last twenty years, I've tried to work out, from language which has often been entirely new and strange to me, what people really meant behind their words, and then to engage and negotiate with them on that basis. It's an approach I've always enjoyed and found entirely at one with the business of reading and writing poetry.

As *Poetry Review* is a magazine I like, I didn't want this jibe to go unanswered, with the implication that perhaps I accepted it. As Michael Mackmin kindly published the poem in *The Rialto* in my original spelling, I'm copying this to him too, with thanks, in case he is puzzled by Pugh's end of term report on it. Perhaps there should be performance-related pay for poetry critics?!

HUGH MACPHERSON
Edinburgh

WHO SAID WHAT TO WHOM

Dear Mr Forbes,

Thank you for publishing my interview with Douglas Dunn in *Poetry Review*. However, please let me draw your attention to two errors in the text: First, my last name appears in misprint in the text as well as on the contents page. For any of the fifteen million Hungarian speakers who may pick up *PR*, my name as printed there will look laughable – which I don't want to be – as well as puzzling: few, if any, will recognize me. My last name is correctly: Dósa, with a single forward stroke instead of twin dots.

Second, on p. 31 in the left-hand side column the paragraph starting with "We can read more and more about..." and ending with "...as 'Scottishness'", belongs to my subsequent question and not to Douglas Dunn's preceding answer. Douglas Dunn didn't say that, and he might protest with justice.

I would be most grateful if you could correct these in the next issue, and thank you again for publishing the interview.

Yours sincerely,
ATTILA DÓSA
School of English
St Andrews

CONTRIBUTORS

Smita Agarwal has recently had residencies at the Scottish Poetry Library and the University of Kent.
Peter Armstrong's first collection is *The Red-Funnelled Boat* (Picador).
Iain Bamforth's latest collection is *Open Workings* (Carcanet).
Ros Barber was shortlisted for this year's Geoffrey Dearmer Prize.
Alan Brownjohn's latest book is a novel, *The Long Shadows* (Dewi Lewis).
Colette Bryce's first collection *The Heel of Bernadette* is due from Picador in January.
Andy Croft's *Nowhere Special* is published by Flambard.

Kwame Dawes' latest collection is *Shook Foil* (Peepal Tree, 1997).
John Gallas's *Resistance is Futile* was published by Carcanet last year.
Philip Gross's latest collection is *The Wasting Game* (Bloodaxe)
Brian Jones' latest collection is *Freeborn John*, Carcanet.
Helen Kitson's *Love Among the Guilty* was published by Bloodaxe in 1995.
Lola Haskins is an American poet who divides her time between the USA and Skipton, Yorkshire.
Roddy Lumsden's *The Book of Love* is due from Bloodaxe in April.
Rod Mengham teaches at Jesus College, Cambridge.
Kevin Murray's first collection *Jaywalking Blues* was published in Australia last year.
Dennis O'Driscoll's new collection is *Weather Permitting* (Anvil).
Ian Parks' first collection is *A Climb through Altered Landscapes* (Blackwater Press).
Lawrence Sail has edited *The New Exeter Book of Riddles* (with Kevin Crossley-Holland, Enitharmon, 1999).
William Scammell's latest collection is *All Set to Fall off the Edge of the World* (Flambard, 1998).
Vernon Scannell's latest book is *The Drums of Morning* (Salamander, 1999).
Gael Turnbull's latest collection is *Rattle of Scree* (Akros, 1997)
Susan Wicks' novel *Little Thing* was published by Faber in 1998.

Eastern Region Artists in Education Training Course

Do you want to gain skills, knowledge and experience in working as an artist in schools? The course for poets, writers, storytellers, visual, media and performing artists will run simultaneously in Essex and Cambridgeshire in September 2000 involving 9 days training and a 10-day residency in a partner school. The course will develop your skills as an artist, increase your knowledge of education and improve your publicity and negotiation skills. For details, send an A5 sae marked 'Artists in Education' to Ronessa Knock, Arts Education Co-ordinator, Cultural Services, Essex County Council, PO Box 47, County Hall, Chelmsford, Essex CM2 6WN, 01245 436015, or Susan Jessop, Cambridge Country Council, Heritage Services, Castle Court, Shire Hall, Cambridgeshire CB3 0AP 01223 718013. Closing date 6 April 2000.